Europe after Stalin
Eisenhower's Three Decisions of March 11, 1953

Ideas and Action Series, No. 3

W.W. Rostow
Europe after Stalin

Eisenhower's Three Decisions of March 11, 1953

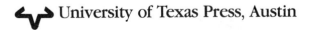 University of Texas Press, Austin

First Edition, 1982

Requests for permission to reproduce material from this work
should be sent to
Permissions, University of Texas Press
Box 7819
Austin, Texas 78712

Library of Congress Cataloging in Publication Data
Rostow, W. W. (Walt Whitman), 1916–
  Europe after Stalin.
  (Ideas and action series)
  Includes bibliographical references and index.
  1. German reunification question (1949–   ).   2. United States—For-
eign relations—Soviet Union.   3. Soviet Union—Foreign relations—
United States.   4. United States—Foreign relations—1953–1961—Deci-
sion making.   5. Eisenhower, Dwight D. (Dwight David), 1890–1969.
6. Rostow, W. W. (Walt Whitman), 1916–   .   I. Title.   II. Series.
  DD257.25.R67   943.087′5   81-19797
ISBN 0-292-72035-1   AACR2
ISBN 0-292-72036-X (pbk.)

This volume was published with the assistance of the Sid W.
Richardson Foundation.

In memory of
Charles Douglas Jackson

Contents

Preface

This is the third in a series of essays centered on the relationship between ideas and action. The first was *Pre-Invasion Bombing Strategy;* the second, *The Division of Europe after World War II: 1946.* Here we are in the world of Cold War diplomacy, as men in Washington and other capitals argue about what, if anything, to do in the wake of Stalin's death.

As for the general theme of the series, I would define ideas as the abstract concepts in the minds of public officials and their advisers which they bring to bear in making decisions. My experiences as both an academic and a public servant have equally driven home over the years this piece of wisdom from George Santayana's *Character and Opinion in the United States:*

> . . . human discourse is intrinsically addressed not to natural existing things but to ideal essences, poetic or logical terms which thought may define and play with. When fortune or necessity diverts our attention from this congenial ideal sport to crude facts and pressing issues, we turn our frail poetic ideas into symbols for those terrible irruptive things. In that paper money of our own stamping, the legal tender of the mind, we are obliged to reckon all the movements and values of the world.

But there is, of course, a good deal more to decisions in public policy than clash and choice among the "frail poetic.

ideas" we create to make simplified sense of an inordinately complex and usually disheveled field of action. A decision is, after all, a choice among perceived alternatives. Ideas play a large role in defining those alternatives, but the choice among them involves other factors. The precise setting and timing of the decision evidently matter. So do questions of power, that is, politics and bureaucratic vested interests. So do personalities—unique human beings, controlled by memories and experiences, dreams and hopes which James Gould Cozzens evoked, in *By Love Possessed*, in a definition of temperament:

> A man's temperament might, perhaps, be defined as the mode or modes of a man's feeling, the struck balance of his ruling desires, the worked-out sum of his habitual predispositions. In themselves, these elements were inscrutable. There were usually too many of them; they were often of irreducible complexity; you could observe only results. . . . The to-be-observed result was a total way of life.

And, as we shall see in the story told here, temperaments thus broadly defined sometimes clash at both the working levels and the highest reaches of government, adding a special wild card to the way history unfolds.

In this effort to illuminate the relationship between ideas and action, I decided to proceed as follows. First, to examine a series of specific decisions taken by particular high public officials at particular times and to reflect on the decision-making process as a whole in a final essay. In the case studies, the decision would be briefly described, including the options which the executive perceived as available to him; the conceptual debate involved in the decision—the more or less pure intellectual content of the process—would be delineated; the larger background of events would be evoked; the interplay between the conceptual debate and the other more mundane forces in play would be examined; the follow-on events and consequences of the decision would be weighed; and some larger lessons of the story would be drawn. Along the way an effort would be made to capture the odd, often adventitious circumstances which entered into the decision and into the way things actually turned out. There are strands of accident and even humor—high, low, or wry—running through a good many of these case studies as well as pratfalls from which even the highest officials are not exempt. Indeed, this is a built-in hazard of the human condition, because decisions are almost always made with imperfect information and foresight, involving a step into the dark. Unlike the first essay of this series, here we are not dealing literally with men groping through "the fog of war," but the image is equally apt for those trying simultaneously to respect the imperatives of the Cold War and to explore the possibilities of breaking out of its grip.

The occasion examined here was, perhaps, the first potentially serious opportunity to seek that reconciliation since Vyacheslav Molotov left the Marshall Plan conference in Paris in July 1947. Although the effort, marked, as we shall see, by uncertainty and ambivalence, failed in 1953 and 1954, it illustrates well the complexity of the problem confronted by those who have sought to find a better way to order international affairs than the dangerous, confrontational format which has dominated the world scene for the past thirty-five years.

I have chosen in this series to examine decisions in which I played some role or which I had an opportunity to observe closely at the time. But, as the reader will perceive, this and the other volumes in the series are not exercises in autobiography. It is simply the case that one has a better chance of capturing something of the relationship between ideas and the other elements determining action if one was reasonably close to events than if the whole complex setting has to be reconstructed from the beginning.

On the other hand, my memory of the circumstances, the material in my files, and my knowledge of some of the actors were patently inadequate. In this and the other case studies, my purpose is to bring to bear what public records, communication with participants, and the literature of published memoirs and works of scholarship can now provide. As in the present volume, there is usually a formidable body of relevant material available.

Certain source or other basic materials, hitherto unpublished or not easily accessible, have been assembled in the appendixes to this book. They are meant to illuminate facets of the decision examined or to capture something of the moods and temper of the time.

Dr. Ted Carpenter, a scholar of this period, has been of invaluable assistance both in mobilizing relevant primary and secondary sources and as a critic of drafts. Our work on this essay was supported by grants from the University Research Institute of the University of Texas at Austin and the National Endowment for the Humanities, whose indispensable help I wish warmly to acknowledge.

I should also like to thank the participants in these events and the scholars who have generously given their time for guidance and criticism: Robert Bowie, Robert A. Divine, Eleanor Lansing Dulles, John S. D. Eisenhower, Milton S. Eisenhower, John W. Ford, Andrew J. Goodpaster, Fred I. Greenstein, John W. Hanes, Jr., Richard H. Immerman, Mrs. C. D. Jackson, George F. Kennan, Phyllis Bernau Macomber, William B. Macomber, Marie McCrum, Paul Nitze, Gary W. Reichard, Elspeth D. Rostow, and Ann Whitman.

Our task was also eased by the knowledgeable assistance of Mrs. Nancy Bressler, at the Mudd Library, Princeton, and by the archivists of the Eisenhower Library at Abilene who reached out to help us.

As on many other occasions, I was aided in multiple ways by Lois Nivens. Frances Knape was most helpful in typing the various drafts.

I should add that this series of essays would not have been

undertaken without the strong encouragement of my wife, Elspeth Davies Rostow, who believed I might usefully reflect on the large central question embedded in those periods in my professional life when I was diverted from strictly academic pursuits.

W. W. Rostow

November 1981
Austin, Texas

Europe after Stalin
Eisenhower's Three Decisions of March 11, 1953

1. The Issues and the Decision

Some six weeks after assuming responsibility, the Eisenhower administration was galvanized, early on Wednesday morning, March 4, 1953, by the news that Stalin was gravely ill. His death was announced on March 6. The debate within the administration on an appropriate course of action reopened, after a fashion, the central issue of the second book in this series: should the United States initiate a proposal to undo the split of Europe and actively propose a democratic unified Germany, within a structure of appropriate security and economic arrangements?

A National Security Council (NSC) directive promptly instructed the CIA to provide an evaluation of the impact of Stalin's death (see Appendix B) and the State Department and C. D. Jackson to recommend appropriate courses of action. Jackson was a special assistant to Eisenhower for what was then called psychological warfare. He and his successor, Nelson Rockefeller, functioned, in fact, as sources of presidential initiatives of substance in foreign policy.

The heart of Jackson's proposal was "A Message to the Soviet Government and the Russian Peoples" from President Eisenhower, which he urged be delivered the day after Stalin's funeral. After discussion with Jackson and at his request, I drafted the message, a rationale for its content, and an outline of possible follow-up actions, during the late afternoon and evening of March 6. The three texts are given in Appendix A.

Among a good many other things, the draft "Message" flatly proposed a quadripartite negotiation and contained this passage:

> The United States shall propose measures for the general control of armaments and special security arrangements for Europe.
>
> The United States shall propose measures for the unification of Germany by free elections as well as proposals designed to end the occupation of Austria. We believe that, within a structure of general and regional security and economic arrangements, a Germany unified by democratic means would constitute a creative force in Europe, without danger to East or West.

The lines of thought that led Jackson and me to suggest this initiative are explored later in this book (pp. 35–41). Briefly, we felt that it was the duty of the United States to hold up to the new Soviet leadership the option of ending the confrontation in the center of Europe and elsewhere, even though the chance of its acceptance was slight; that a pacific stance by the United States at this juncture would maximize the chance for liberalizing changes in Soviet society; that the initiative should be taken promptly for maximum effect, among other reasons, to preempt a possible Soviet peace offensive; and that the initiative could be mounted in ways which might reinforce rather than obtrude upon the European Defense Community (EDC) initiative, since the bargaining position of the West in a negotiation with Moscow about Germany would be stronger with EDC in hand than without it. Letters from Eisenhower to the major European leaders were drafted, explaining his initiative, to be delivered before the event (also in Appendix A).

The concept of such a presidential statement and its broad contents were explored on March 6 (before the text was drafted) in a meeting including Jackson and Emmet Hughes from the White House, Charles Bohlen and Paul Nitze from the State Department. (Appendix C presents extracts from a chronological account of events, as I saw them, assembled at Jackson's request and dispatched to him on May 11, 1953.) Although the discussion was indecisive, there appeared to be agreement that any meaningful statement by the president would have to include a concrete proposal for a high-level four-power meeting. On Monday, March 9, however, it was evident that there would be quite significant opposition from the State Department. This emerged when Hughes, at Jackson's direction, showed the three documents to Bohlen and Nitze.

The objections of the State Department to an early presidential speech were crystallized in a memorandum of March 11 transmitted by the undersecretary of state (Walter Bedell Smith) to Jackson and others at the undersecretary level in the foreign affairs community (see Appendix D). It constituted the brief presented to Secretary John Foster Dulles by his aides for the NSC meeting of that day and contained four main points:

1. A presidential speech should be postponed "until an important opportunity arises."

2. No meeting of foreign ministers should be advocated until U.S. proposals had been formulated.

3. The proposal of a foreign ministers meeting without prior consultation with major allies would be divisive.

4. ". . . a meeting of Foreign Ministers would indefinitely delay progress on EDC. No action could be expected by European Governments on EDC pending outcome and evaluation of the Ministers' meeting."

On the ninth it had been decided to postpone a formal discussion of the matter with the president until Wednesday, March 11, since Dulles would be out of Washington until late afternoon on the tenth. On his return, Dulles received the Jackson proposal, conferred with his State Department colleagues, and breakfasted with Jackson early on the morning of the eleventh. He said he found Jackson's proposed initiative "intriguing" but had certain reservations which he did not discuss with Jackson at the time.

Under circumstances described in Appendix C, George Kennan, recently declared *persona non grata* as ambassador to the Soviet Union, was brought to Washington by Jackson. They conferred on March 10. Kennan gave Jackson's proposal strong intellectual and moral support, although he was not then in a position of influence in Washington. As we shall see, Kennan's position on Germany and Europe had evolved in a rather dramatic way since 1945–1947 (pp. 41–45, below). Kennan told Jackson that the proposed initiative required great clarity concerning its implications for Germany on the part of two men: the president and the secretary of state. If this condition were fulfilled, there was no need to worry excessively about other opinions in Washington or about the short period of excitement in the foreign offices in London, Paris, and Bonn. Kennan expressed his faith that Washington would respond with vigor and unity to the initiative, as it had to the Marshall Plan proposal, and that our allies would come along without much difficulty.

The initial showdown came in a two-hour NSC meeting on March 11, starting at 10:30 A.M. The records of that meeting have not been declassified. The only account I can find is Jackson's report to me as he emerged from the meeting, which I summarized soon afterward as follows (see Appendix C):

> Rostow saw Jackson again as he emerged from the NSC meeting at about 12:30 P.M. Jackson announced that he did not know whether he was a man "carrying a shield or being carried upon it." He reported that
> (a) he had had his full day in court;
> (b) the President, remembering his experience with previous four-power meetings, was not enthusiastic about the Council of Foreign Ministers;
> (c) Dulles took the position that our relations with

France and Britain would be damaged by a unilateral initiative of this kind; that the governments of [Alcides] de Gasperi, [Konrad] Adenauer and [René] Mayer would fall in a week; and that EDC would be postponed, if not destroyed. It was, nevertheless, agreed that a Presidential statement should be made and made soon, and that the bulk of the text as drafted was suitable. . . .

It was further decided that the references to Korea would be expanded and a truce in Korea would be made even more clearly a condition for further movement toward the larger objectives of peace than the original draft had provided. Jackson was instructed to prepare a new text in the sense of the meeting.

While Jackson was at lunch on Wednesday, March 11, Rostow redrafted the message as instructed by Jackson. [The modifications in the original draft are included in Appendix A.] The essential device was to hold up a vision of the specific long-range objectives of American diplomacy but to make the negotiations designed to achieve that vision contingent upon a prior Korean settlement.

At the close of business on March 11, Eisenhower dispatched a cable to Winston Churchill (see Appendix A) who had proposed a prompt Big Four summit meeting. It contained the three basic decisions which were to shape U.S. policy on this matter over the next year: a Big Four summit was rejected; Eisenhower indicated his desire to make a speech soon "giving to the world some promise of hope"; it held out the possibility of a Western summit meeting including the U.K. and "probably the French."

A presidential statement of the kind envisaged on March 11 was not, in fact, made until five weeks had passed, exchanges had taken place with the major European leaders, and some fourteen drafts had been formulated.[1] Three factors account for the delay:

1. The seizure of the peace initiative by Georgi M. Malenkov, starting with his statement before the Supreme Soviet,

published on March 16: "At the present time there is no disputed or unresolved question that cannot be settled peacefully by mutual agreement of the interested countries. This applies to our relations with all states, including the United States of America."[2]

2. Dulles' anxiety that nothing be done at American initiative to interfere with the passage of EDC, then before the Continental parliaments.

3. Dulles' skepticism about negotiations with the Soviet Union and anxiety about major presidential pronouncements on foreign policy—an anxiety that was to emerge on several occasions over his tenure in office.

Eisenhower, after considerable uncertainty, finally decided to proceed with the speech despite Dulles' lack of enthusiasm for it, although the latter's initial flat opposition gradually eroded as it became clear that the Soviet peace offensive was, in any case, holding up forward movement on EDC and generating political pressures on the Western European governments for a positive response. The president delivered his famous speech before the American Society of Newspaper Editors (see Appendix E). It was published in *Pravda* and *Izvestia*, along with a temperate but quite precise critique; widely acclaimed elsewhere; and defined Eisenhower before the world, in his first major presidential pronouncement, as a statesman actively seeking peace. Most analysts of the period would agree with Sherman Adams' assessment that, however meager its direct policy consequences, "it was the most effective speech of Eisenhower's public career, and certainly one of the highlights of his presidency."[3] Two days later Dulles delivered a speech of his own, covering similar ground but considerably harsher in tone—a fact duly noted in Soviet commentaries (see Appendix E).

The president's speech, as delivered, dealt with the German question in much the style of the draft prepared in the wake of the March 11 NSC meeting. That is, a broad vision of what American policy ultimately sought was held up, with action toward it dependent on the prior settlement of other issues, notably Korea:

> We are ready not only to press forward with the present plans for closer unity of the nations of western Europe but also, upon that foundation, to strive to foster a broader European community, conducive to the free movement of persons, of trade, and of ideas.
> This community would include a free and united Germany, with a government based upon free and secret ballot.
> This free community and the full independence of the East European nations could mean the end of the present unnatural division of Europe.

In the wake of Eisenhower's speech, the diplomatic channels became active, but they were crosscut by a number of events including, first, a softening of Soviet policy in East Germany, then riots in June. It was not until January 1954 that the foreign ministers met in Moscow, by which time any flexibility on the German question that may (or may not) have existed in the Soviet government earlier in the year had evaporated.

In terms of concept, three differences in perspective had to be resolved between Stalin's death and Eisenhower's April 16 speech: differences between Eisenhower's and Dulles' views of what the moment in history called for; differences between Jackson and the State Department on what U.S. course of action was most likely to hold the alliance together; and, to a degree, differences on German policy itself. There were also differences on policy in Asia that had to be resolved within the government.

Before probing these differences in concept in relation to the many other factors at work over the critical five weeks, it may be useful to turn back and examine the setting in which the debate arose as well as the background to it, including the background which shaped the perspectives of some of the major and minor players.

2. The Background: Europe, the U.S.S.R., and the U.S.

First, the background in Europe which rendered the EDC such a critical issue in alliance policy in the late winter and early spring of 1953.

As early as March 1947, France and Britain signed a pact of mutual defense, the Dunkirk Treaty. As it became clear that European recovery would proceed in an atmosphere of Soviet hostility, with substantial Soviet forces on the Elbe confronting a virtual ground force vacuum, the Anglo-French arrangement was joined by Belgium, the Netherlands, and Luxembourg in the Brussels Pact of March 1948. Stalin's Berlin blockade of 1948–1949 heightened anxieties about European defense, yielding the NATO treaty, embracing seven additional countries, including Canada and the United States. The treaty was ratified by the Senate in July 1949. At that stage NATO was envisaged as a tripwire or plate glass window which would guarantee American engagement in case of Soviet attack. It was, in effect, a symbol of mutual commitment with the U.S. Strategic Air Command, exercising a nuclear monopoly, judged to be a sufficient deterrent against a Soviet unleashing of its ground forces.

This concept was shaken by the Soviet explosion of a nuclear weapon in September 1949 and the North Korean assault on South Korea in June 1950. These events suggested between them that Moscow, within the framework of a nuclear stalemate, might be prepared to exploit its ground force superiority in Europe. Many drew a direct parallel between Korea and Germany: divided countries with a strong military force in the Communist sector confronting weak ground forces across the line of the occupation zones. The shock of the North Korean attack, whether correctly interpreted or not as a possible forerunner of Soviet action elsewhere, was profound in Europe as well as in the United States. A consensus emerged that NATO would have to be given sufficient substance to defend Western Europe on the ground.

Thus, the difficult issue of German rearmament was first posed. German rearmament was a military necessity if a sufficient ground force were to be developed in Western Europe to deter the Soviet conventional strength—for Britain, France, Italy, and the United States were, in different ways, under political and economic inhibitions which precluded the development of a sufficient counterforce on the Central Front without a substantial German contribution.

For Germany the problem was difficult for other reasons. It was believed by some that the arming of West Germany might be regarded as an act sufficiently provocative to bring on war. Others feared it would foreclose the possibility of negotiations for German unity with the Russians. In another direction, it was felt that the revival of militarism might set back the still weak but gathering forces in West Germany which had been working toward the development of democracy at home and a Western orientation abroad. Nevertheless, under Adenauer's guidance, the move was accepted in principle. Adenauer—the incarnation of much in the Germany which had been lost when Prussia came to domination in the wake of the Revolution of 1848—may, in his heart, have been somewhat ambivalent about a united Germany. But he certainly believed that the only safe course for Germany was to associate itself inextricably with the West and move toward unity as part of a strong Western European base supported by the United States. This judgment was based not merely on an assessment of Germany's limited bilateral bargaining strength vis-à-vis Russia but also on a fear of the course his country-men might pursue if they once again moved on their own in the arena of European and world power.

Adenauer's position on this matter and his capacity to carry his countrymen were tested by Moscow in 1952. Evidently wishing to avoid the militarization of West Germany within the NATO structure, the Soviet Union launched on March 10 a proposal for a Four Power Peace Conference which would define the framework for a unified demilitarized Germany. Adenauer believed, no doubt correctly, that the timing of the Soviet initiative was meant to break the momentum of the movement of the Federal Republic of Germany (FRG) to full sovereignty and feared the consequences of leaving Germany a military vacuum. In this he was supported by the Western powers. In a joint response of March 25 they agreed to insist on free all-German elections, under United Nations supervision, and the right of a future German government to choose its friends and allies. The reference to U.N. supervision of German elections was, at the time, a quasi-operational matter. After a series of exchanges in 1951 between Adenauer and Otto Grotewohl, the East German prime minister, the U.N. General Assembly formed a commission to define the conditions for the holding of a free all-German election. West Germany accepted. Soviet acceptance of the presence of the commission to do its work in East Germany became the touchstone for the seriousness of Moscow's intentions. The commission was banned from East Germany. And the terms of a Soviet note of August 29, 1952, appeared to justify the Western position. It called for elections only after a peace treaty had been signed by a German government formed on a fifty-fifty East-West basis. Thus, Adenauer was able to proceed in good conscience and with majority support.

Nevertheless, some Social Democrats felt the Soviet initiative of March 1952 had not been properly explored, whatever its tactical motives may have been; and many Germans were more skeptical than Adenauer of a long-run strategy of unity with Western Europe and the Atlantic world and less frightened of negotiation with Moscow. But the majority were persuaded to follow Adenauer's lead as a tactic, if for no other reason than that the West still had considerable to offer Germany—and was willing to make the offer—whereas Moscow was evidently not prepared to offer the prize of unity on tolerable political terms. And psychologically West Germans in the early 1950s were primarily absorbed in the process of economic reconstruction and revival. It was still some time before they would be prepared to look out on the world and define their destiny on the European and world scenes.

In France, of course, the reemergence of German military strength set in motion profound instinctive fears, despite the existence of NATO. Partly to diminish those fears, the United States, after searching congressional and public debate, made in 1951 the commitment to maintain four divisions in Europe—a momentous decision in terms of previous American reactions to French requests for a security guarantee, stretching back to Versailles.

To the British, NATO had several attractive features. At the time, the British commitment to the European continent was essentially in naval and air strength, and this fitted British plans and military thought. Moreover, the organization of NATO gave the British great influence through General Hastings Ismay's role in the secretary-generalship and General Bernard Montgomery's command over the ground forces. As an organization, NATO had many of the advantages of the Supreme Headquarters, Allied Expeditionary Force (SHAEF), during the Second World War. Finally, London found satisfaction in the wholehearted manner in which Canada could participate in NATO arrangements. For Canadians an enterprise which attracted the support of the United States, Britain, and France was the optimum setting in which to play an active role on the world scene, given the nature of Canadian social and political life. It is fair to say that NATO, as organized and set in motion in 1949–1952, set up fewer conflicts and strains in London than in any other major capital.

NATO rapidly gathered strength in 1951–1952 as Congress agreed to station the American divisions, Eisenhower built Supreme Headquarters, Allied Powers, Europe (SHAPE), and substantial American aid helped build the infrastructure, that is, the airfield, logistical and communications base of the enterprise. Moreover, Germany appeared to be moving slowly but steadily toward the assumption of responsibility for a major ground force contribution; and, generally, the will of Europe to make a substantial sacrifice in order to deter Soviet ground force troops seemed beyond question.

But a critical issue remained: what form should the German ground force contribution take? The formula that appeared for a time to reconcile this requirement with fears of a national German army came from France, and it came, quite particularly, from Jean Monnet.[4] He perceived, on the Sunday of the North Korean attack, that the war in Asia, with all its repercussions, might upset the schedule for bringing to life the Schuman Plan, then at a critical stage. As the second half of 1950 unfolded, it became apparent that France could not resist indefinitely a large German contribution to European defense. Monnet proposed, therefore, that the German forces become part of a Continental European defense structure administered, like the Coal and Steel Community, by a supranational institution. He suggested the concept to René Pleven, then French prime minister, who tentatively laid it before the French parliament on October 24, 1950. After much complex negotiation and many vicissitudes, the EDC treaty was signed in Paris on May 27, 1952, but it still had to face the parliament. In France, the integration of armies proved vastly more intractable than the integration of policies toward coal and steel. The most visceral strands in French nationalism surfaced—as much, or perhaps more, by the proposed integration of French forces as by the emergence of large German forces. In the face of opposition, the supporters of EDC in the French government delayed a parliamentary showdown for many months, but the treaty was laid before the National Assembly in January 1953. As Monnet notes: "For more than a year, the dispute about EDC had underlain all political attitudes in France, in the parties, in Parliament, and in the Government itself."[5] That was where the matter stood in Paris—precarious and undecided—when Stalin died on March 6.

Although, as noted earlier, the question of EDC posed some problems for Adenauer, on balance it represented a step forward for Germany in the recovery of a place of full equality in the Western community; and it conformed to the majority judgment that Germany's destiny, including the possibility of ultimate German unification, lay in intimate association with a strong and united West.

In his first major move as secretary of state, Dulles toured Western Europe between January 31 and February 8, 1953. Accompanied by Harold Stassen, he visited Rome, Paris, London, Bonn, The Hague, Brussels, and Luxembourg. His primary objective, aside from feeling out the diplomatic ground, was to urge the European governments to complete ratification of EDC.

Dulles arrived in Bonn on February 5 and spoke with Social Democratic leaders as well as with Adenauer and his government colleagues.[6] He argued that European integration had caught the imagination of the American people and that EDC and a strong Western Europe associated with the United States were the optimum basis for movement toward German unity; and he urged that the treaty be passed definitively on its third reading by the Bundestag. On March 19, the Bundestag accepted the treaty with a somewhat larger majority than in its second reading, and the Federal Republic of Germany became its first signatory.

Plunged as he was into the diplomacy and politics of EDC in the several capitals, it is not difficult to understand Dulles' uneasiness on March 11 about presidential statements and initiatives toward an all-German settlement. For Dulles, Stalin's death, and all the attendant fuss, was intruding on serious business.

Stalin's death occurred at a particular moment not only in the affairs of the West but also in the rhythm of relations between the Soviet Union and the world beyond. He died when the phase of postwar reconstruction was over and his initial exertions to expand Soviet power in the context of postwar disarray in Eurasia had just about reached their limits. In a manner resonant of Russian history, he had pressed first in the West and, then, when frustrated, turned to apparent opportunities in the East.

During the summer of 1946, Stalin increased Soviet pressure against Turkey by diplomacy and threat, in Greece by supporting substantial guerrilla warfare via Bulgaria and Yugoslavia and in Italy and France by vigorous Communist party efforts to gain parliamentary power. Meanwhile, the process of stabilizing Germany as two organized entities proceeded. In 1947 Stalin was thrown on the defensive by Truman's counterattack. He responded to the Truman Doctrine and the Marshall Plan by accelerating the movement toward total control in the East, symbolized by the creation of the Cominform in September 1947. He succeeded in Prague (February 1948) but failed in Belgrade, where Tito's defection was announced in June 1948. The Communist effort in Greece then collapsed, the election in April 1948 stabilized democratic Italy, and France found a group of center parties capable of governing, albeit uncertainly, and containing domestic Communist strength. The deadlock in the Berlin Control Council, already two years old, was dramatized by the Soviet walkout on March 20, 1948, which set the stage for the blockade, begun on March 31.

This phase of Soviet consolidation in Eastern Europe ended with the effort to expel the West from Berlin, which was defeated by the airlift in the winter of 1948–49. In the West this interacting process yielded, as we have noted, the Brussels Pact (March 1948), NATO (signed April 1949), and the creation (May 1949) of a Federal Republic of Germany, including, for economic purposes, the Western zones of Berlin—an act which symbolized and confirmed the Western intent to resist further Soviet expansion.

In the course of 1946, the negotiations for a truce in China also broke down and all-out civil war began. In 1946 Stalin probably advised against an all-out effort by the Communists to seize power, but, once Mao was well started, he was backed by Stalin from 1947 to 1949. Communist policy in Asia formally changed in the course of 1947, ambitious new objectives being enunciated by Andrei A. Zhdanov at the founding meeting of the Cominform in September. Open guerrilla warfare began in Indochina as early as November 1946, in Burma in April 1948, in Malaya in June of that year, and in Indonesia and the Philippines in the autumn. The Indian and Japanese Communist parties, with less scope for guerrilla action, nevertheless sharply increased their militancy in 1948. As final victory was won in China in November 1949, Mao's political-military strategy was openly commended by the Cominform to the Communist parties in those areas where guerrilla operations were under way. Stalin and Mao met early in 1950 and confirmed the ambitious Asian strategy, planning its climax, in response to Kim Il Sung's appeal, in the form of the North Korean invasion of South Korea, which took place at the end of June 1950.

The American and United Nations response to the invasion of South Korea, the landings at Inchon, the march to the Yalu, the Chinese Communist entrance into the war, and the successful U.N. defense against massive Chinese assault in April and May 1951 at the thirty-eighth parallel brought this phase of military and quasi-military Communist effort throughout Asia to a gradual end. Neither Moscow nor Peking was willing to undertake all-out war or even accept the cost of a continued Korean offensive. And elsewhere the bright Communist hopes of 1946 and 1947 had dimmed. Nowhere in Asia was Mao's success repeated. Indonesia, Burma, and the Philippines largely overcame their guerrillas. At great cost to Britain, the Malayan guerrillas were contained and driven back. Only in Indochina, where French colonialism offered a seedbed as fruitful as postwar China, was there real Communist momentum. When Stalin died the Korean negotiations had been indecisively under way for some twenty months and China, rather than the Soviet Union, was most active in support of the Viet Minh.

Like his postwar offensive, Stalin too had been winding down for some time. From the quite consistent accounts of his daughter Svetlana and Khrushchev, Stalin's health was failing progressively in 1951–1952, and with this came a heightening of his pathological distrust of all around him. Stalin's last days, his macabre death, and the Byzantine maneuvers it set in motion, climaxed by the brutal execution of Lavrenti P. Beria in July, all have the flavor of an earlier century. But, quite particularly, Stalin died at a moment of internal tension centered on the so-called doctors' plot, announced on January 13, 1953. It had all the earmarks of an inner struggle for power, possibly to be accompanied by purges evocative of the 1930s. Among those who followed Soviet events, the period between mid January and early March was one of considerable concern about the course that that nation was likely to take in the time ahead.

As an era was ending in Moscow, a page was also turned in Washington with the arrival of the first Republican president since the departure of Herbert Hoover. In an oral history interview in 1970, Charles Bohlen, looking back on the early days of the Eisenhower administration, observed: "In fact, I used to think to myself that the Republicans came into the State Department rather like a wagon train going into hostile Indian territory, and every night they'd group their wagons around the fire."[7] Knowing both some of the Republicans who had recently come to responsibility and some of the older State Department hands—and having the privilege of observing their interaction in the early days—I can attest that Bohlen's image was apt, but the suspicion was mutual.

After all, this was the first Republican administration in twenty years. Its members arrived in Washington after a campaign in which Korea, Communism, and corruption were major directions of attack on the Truman administration. The Hiss affair was still a corrosive and vivid memory. Even those Republicans who took a more sophisticated and tolerant view of the outgoing Democrats felt authentically that their predecessors were burned out, and it was time for a fresh start in new directions. Dulles, in particular, was extremely sensitive—in Eisenhower's view, occasionally oversensitive—to the possible charge that he was merely carrying forward Acheson's policies, notably in Asia, which he had been so recently denouncing with vigor. But both Eisenhower and Dulles were understandably anxious to avoid the exacerbated relations between the executive branch and Congress on foreign policy which marked the latter Truman years.[8]

Moreover, the old hands with whom the newly arrived Republicans had to deal had lived most, if not all, of their professional lives under Democratic administrations, were probably voting Democrats, and were judged, prima facie, to be antagonistic to the new team. And there was something in that view. Jackson, for example, was initially regarded in the State Department as a somewhat superficial sloganeer without a serious grounding in the realities of diplomacy. When I talked to two of my old friends in the State Department in the immediate aftermath of Stalin's death, their reaction was that the White House should "do nothing" on the grounds that the new boys were likely to do something irresponsible. Quite soon, however, their professional instincts took over. For example, Nitze, director of the Policy Planning Staff, was soon working in reasonable harmony with the White House speech drafters. But it took a good deal longer for the State Department as a whole to get over the first meeting of Dulles with department officials: "Dulles's words were as cold and raw as the weather that February day. He said that he was going to insist that every member of the department extend not just loyalty but 'positive loyalty.' He did not define the difference, but his intent was clear. It was a declaration by the Secretary of State that the department was indeed suspect. The remark disgusted some Foreign Service officers, infuriated others, and displeased even those who were looking forward to the new administration."[9]

There was another complicating dimension to all this: the strong McCarthyite mood in Congress which came sharply into focus with the nomination of Bohlen to the post of ambassador to the Soviet Union.[10] Bohlen was one of the most respected senior members of the Foreign Service, as well as a man of charm, vivacity, and courage. Rather to his surprise, he was nominated on January 23, 1953, to succeed Kennan. The proceedings in the Senate gradually built up into an ugly, harrowing affair, with Joseph McCarthy challenging the 15 to 0 favorable vote of the Foreign Affairs Committee and demanding the withdrawal of the nomination. Dulles, extremely sensitive to the Republican right wing but also conscious that the morale of his department was at stake, was much concerned. Eisenhower, however, stood firm; Senators Taft and Sparkman were permitted to read Bohlen's security file and vouched for the harmlessness of its contents; and on April 4 Bohlen left for Moscow.[11] But the first month of the period we are considering—March 4 to April 16, 1953—was suffused by this controversy with the special intensity that Washington, essentially an inbred company town, can generate in such matters. As one who was in Washington quite often over these weeks, I can attest that the Bohlen affair, in all its ramifications, was an obsessive subject for discussion in the office corridors and at the cocktail parties of the community.

Aside from these human and institutional tensions, larger considerations helped shape the setting in which Eisenhower finally decided to give his speech. The nation had gone through an exceedingly hard time during the Korean War: the initial setback, MacArthur's brilliant riposte at Inchon, the surge of hubris that led to the movement north toward the Yalu, the unexpected entrance of the Chinese Communists into the war, the firing of MacArthur with its attendant bitter debate, the little-noted defensive victories of April and May 1951 leading to the opening of truce talks, and then month after month of indecisive combat at the thirty-eighth parallel, with substantial casualties and little progress in the negotiations. All this was heightened by a regime of irksome price and wage controls. Truman's approval rating, which had fallen as low as 24 percent during the MacArthur controversy, stood at only 31 percent when he left office. As the nation was to learn again during the struggle in Southeast Asia, its style and instincts did not accommodate easily to limited, protracted war. The hope that Eisenhower could end that war was a major, but by no means unique, reason for his victory in November 1952. In the wake of Stalin's death, Eisenhower understood viscerally and correctly that the war-weary nation yearned for peace and a more hopeful future.

This judgment converged with the basic budgetary and military strategy the new administration had adopted. Those who dominated the Republican party looked to a reduction in the role of the federal government in American life as the necessary condition for retaining the sort of society to which they were attached. For twenty years, in political impotence or active opposition, they had watched the absolute size of federal expenditures rise—first during the New Deal, then during the Second World War, and finally during the Korean War. Not only had they watched with disapproval and fear the extension of federal powers, along with the expanded welfare and control functions of the state, but, also, at times of war and rapid rearmament, they had seen and felt the related dangers of inflation and direct administrative control over prices and raw materials. Above all, it was the aspiration of a substantial group of Republicans to undo these believed evils when political power was regained and to move American society back toward an older balance between government and private capitalism—and, in a wider sense, between government and private life—which they found more congenial. They were convinced that minimum essential American interests could be protected with diminished direct responsibility and at less cost. Further, many Republicans had convinced themselves that the nation's costly military and foreign policy—including the Korean War—was the result of incompetent meddling in the world rather than of an inescapable, if belated, effort to protect straightforward American interests. With authentic passion, they sought to cut the federal budget, to reduce the scope of federal power in the economy, and to reduce the nation's commitments on the world scene.

Thus in December 1952, when key members of the new administration gathered for three days on the cruiser *Helena* with Eisenhower en route from Korea, the central task was defined in terms of the Great Equation—how to equate minimum needed military strength with maximum economic strength. Wrestling with this definition of the problem, the strategists defined their objectives in the following two categories.

> *In economic policy:* To remove controls as rapidly as possible. To bring down the cost of the federal government by a rigorous extirpation of wasteful and unnecessary services and by removing the government from areas and functions that properly belong to the free market. Thus to balance the budget as soon as possible. To curb excessive credit.
>
> *For the national security:* To liquidate the Korean War at once, accepting the stalemate. To proceed with a thoroughgoing examination of the military establishment and of the strategic estimate, as the matter of topmost priority on taking office, in the expectation that great savings would

result. Eisenhower made a strong point on the rapid obsoles-cence of weapons as a result of technical breakthroughs and insisted that military forces and strategy must be reshaped around these new weapons for what he called "the Long Haul."[12]

In human terms, this definition of the task emerged from the interplay of three views within the Eisenhower team. First, there was the view of what might be called the mid-western Republicans. They were not isolationists in the sense that they sought to reverse radically and promptly the exist-ing national commitments beyond the hemisphere, but their minds were strongly colored by isolationist images and con-ceptions from the past. They did not accept with sympathy and understanding the sequence of modern history which had engaged the United States so deeply around the whole periphery of Eurasia and on the European continent itself. The names of Alfred Thayer Mahan, Elihu Root, Charles Evans Hughes, and Henry Stimson evoked little, if anything, in their memory or experience.

Second, there was the view of the eastern Republicans who were in part linked to the internationalist Republican tradition but either were committed to respect the midwestern view or shared in some measure its economic presuppositions.

Third, there was the view of the liberal (predominantly eastern) Republicans—mainly responsible for Eisenhower's nomination—who felt that the Truman administration had become sluggish, unimaginative, and excessively defensive in dealing with the nation's military and foreign policy problems and who looked to new programs and initiatives. Although they were eager to explore ways of protecting and advancing the national interest at reduced cost, in their hearts these men did not doubt that the nation could spend more on external affairs without risking capitalism and democracy.

While much of the rhetoric of Eisenhower's initial term was fashioned from the conceptions of the third group, the framework of policy was set by the first, holding as they did what Lenin might have called "the commanding heights" within the executive branch: Treasury, Defense, and the Budget Bureau, with George Humphrey at Treasury clearly the leader. And, within these conflicting dispensations of language and money, the second group sought day-to-day compromises which would prevent the gap from becoming overt or excessive.

When the full cabinet gathered in the Hotel Commodore in New York on January 12, 1953, to hear the president-elect read the draft of his first inaugural address, among the major themes discussed were the budget and the rate at which it could be reduced, given the position in which it was left toward the close of the Korean War, and the appropriate timing for the removal of the price and wage controls placed on the economy during the Korean War.

In retrospect, two things are clear about the administration's conception of the Great Equation. First, maximum economic strength was viewed primarily as the maximum degree of freedom for the private sectors of the economy, minimum tax revenues, and, hopefully, a relatively stable price level. Other concepts of economic strength occasionally entered into the administration's thought—for example, the notion that high levels of output in, say, aluminum, required for the civilian economy, also increased long-run military potential. But, operationally, strength was normally equated with minimal administrative intervention by the government into the economy and with reduced taxation. Second, the assumption was initially made that the new military technology would cheapen the costs of military defense. This was a somewhat static conception, in which a kind of once-and-for-all substitution of nuclear weapon delivery capabilities for manpower was envisaged. This view did not embrace a realistic vision of the costly succession of new weapons systems—each leaving a prompt trail of obsolescence—

which was just over the horizon. Eisenhower understood this process better than some in his administration.

Once in power, certain inescapable facts of the world arena in which the nation lived and operated and certain inescapable requirements of national security were respected. But in the formative months, when policy wavered in the councils of the executive branch, there was Taft to remind them of the meaning of the Republican victory:

> The President opened the meeting with a statement on foreign affairs and the new military policy. When he had finished, there were explanations of the new budget and national defense by [George] Humphrey, [Joseph] Dodge, and [Roger] Kyes. All three pointed out that although the new administration had been in office barely three months, it was already giving a new direction to Federal spending. A beginning, at least, they said, had been made in reducing Truman's budget estimates.
>
> The full import of their words was nevertheless that heavy military spending would continue, that more deficits lay ahead and that the first Republican budget would be out of balance. When this hit Robert A. Taft, he went off like a bomb.
>
> The sedate discussion was rent by his hard, metallic voice. Fairly shouting and banging his fist on the Cabinet table, Taft declared that all the efforts of the Eisenhower Administration to date had merely produced the net result of continued spending on the same scale as the Truman Administration. Unless the inconceivable step of raising taxes was taken, he said, the new budget—the budget for the fiscal year 1954— would carry a large deficit. He denounced the budget total as one that exceeded 20 per cent of the national income, a limit Taft thought high enough.
>
> The President was taken aback as Taft barked out a prediction that the first Eisenhower budget would drive a wedge between the administration and the economy-minded Republicans in Congress and drag the party to defeat in the 1954 elections.

> "The one primary thing we promised the American people," he shouted, "was a reduction of expenditures. Now you're taking us right down the same road Truman traveled. It's a repudiation of everything we promised in the campaign."
>
> Taft said that he could see no prospect of future reductions so long as emphasis was placed upon military preparedness for which, he said, funds could be spent without limit.[13]

Thus, in 1953, as the nation was confronted by the expensive consequences of the revolutionary forces at work in weapons technology and in the underdeveloped areas, its policy was controlled by a powerful and purposeful thrust to reduce the size of the federal budget.

Eisenhower's instinct to reach out for the possibility of peace, like that of all the other post-1945 American presidents, was no doubt rooted in fundamental values and aspirations. In his case this instinct was heightened by a thoroughly professional knowledge of the nature of nuclear weapons and the irrationality of their use except to deter their use by others. But a strand of budgetary concern was also present. As Eisenhower encountered opposition, in the course of drafting his speech, to a peaceful gesture in general and, as we shall see, to limiting the preconditions in Asia for a settlement in Korea and a negotiation on Germany, the budgetary costs of continued conflict and confrontation were much on his mind.

3. American Perceptions of the Soviet Union and the Death of Stalin

Over the three decades between the October Revolution and Truman's acceptance of a state of Cold War in 1947, the average American's view of the Soviet Union and of the purposes of its leaders varied widely. Despite oscillations in mood, the predominant American view was a mixture of two elements: considerable ignorance and a vague conviction that the Soviet Union was an evil dictatorship dedicated to the destruction of the basic values and institutions of Western civilization. This fixed—and by no means wholly inaccurate—image did not, of course, exhaust the range of American attitudes toward and perspectives on the Soviet Union. There was, for example, widespread apathy about the Soviet Union in the 1920s, except for a small group of Americans fascinated by the "Communist experiment." Essentially as a depression measure, the Soviet Union was recognized in 1933 in order to encourage the expansion of American foreign trade. And in the 1930s the drama of the first two Five-Year Plans, against the background of Western economic crisis, stirred a wider interest and a somewhat enlarged sympathy; but this mood was radically altered by the Soviet purges, the Soviet-German pact, and Soviet policy during the early stage of the Second World War, notably the invasion of Finland. The strong anti-Soviet sentiment of 1939–1940 gave way, of course, to a more benign, but still wary, view after

Hitler's invasion of the Soviet Union in June 1941 and the gallant, costly, but ultimately successful struggle of the Russian peoples.

Within the United States government and in American intellectual life, only a few knew a good deal about the Soviet Union. By a kind of minor miracle, the Foreign Service produced several men of remarkable perception and scholarship in Russian affairs, notably George Kennan and Charles Bohlen. In the universities, Geroid T. Robinson at Columbia and Michael Karpovich at Harvard carried forward the study of Russian history and began to apply to its Soviet phase the most refined tools of Western research. They fostered a second, much larger generation of Soviet scholars. In addition, there was a steady flow of books and articles by journalists, expatriates, Communist sympathizers, naïve and enthusiastic observers of the Soviet scene, and—especially after 1929, when Stalin declared himself for the policy of "socialism in one country"—disappointed former members of the international Communist movement.

Despite these elements of study, reporting, advocacy, and polemics, it is fair to say that when the Second World War came solid knowledge of the workings of Soviet society, the evolution of Soviet policy, and the relation of the Soviet phase to the rest of Russian history was confined to a handful of American citizens. The Second World War accelerated the development of this knowledge, because, among other reasons, most of the younger men equipped to deal with the Russian language were put to work under forced draft in various agencies of the government, notably in the research and analysis branch of the Office of Strategic Services, over which Professor Robinson presided, permitting not the slightest dilution of scholarly standards. And after the war, at Columbia, Harvard, and elsewhere, the training of scholars in Soviet affairs, both for work in government and for teaching, increased remarkably.

Meanwhile, Stalin's postwar posture clarified; and by 1947, both inside and outside the government, an appreciation of the status of Soviet society along the lines of George Kennan's "X" article—"The Sources of Soviet Conduct"—represented something of a consensus among the widening, but still statistically small, group concerned with the gathering struggle against Stalin's purposes. That view regarded the Soviet Union as an effective working society, capable of offering to those within it a mixture of positive incentives and terror sufficient to yield effective military and economic performance. It accepted as fact a level of Soviet investment high enough, combined with sufficient organizational skill, to assure that the Soviet Union would continue to grow as an industrial economy. It accepted as fact the built-in hostility of Soviet leaders toward the non-Communist world and their operational intent to extend their power as far as their own strengths and weaknesses and the resistance of the outside world would permit. It accepted also the fact that Soviet society was undergoing a series of internal changes away from the social and political norms of the 1920s and early 1930s, but the timing and significance for the external world of those changes and the degree to which they would prove consistent with the maintenance of Communism were matters of some debate. Finally, there was agreement that Moscow was likely to be reasonably cautious in the use of Soviet military force in pursuit of its expansionary postwar objectives. It was on the basis of some such assessment that the Truman counteroffensive was launched early in 1947.

The Soviet acquisition of atomic weapons by September 1949 revealed an intent and a capability to apply the new technology with a swiftness somewhat beyond that which most observers had held likely, and a change began to take place in the American assessment of Soviet purposes. The notion of a generalized but militarily cautious program of aggression toward the non-Communist world gave way to the conception that the Soviets might be engaged in a systematic buildup of modern military strength, looking toward a showdown which might come when the curves of Soviet and Americn military capabilities crossed—a date estimated to be round about 1952. An estimate of this kind was incorporated in NSC 68, completed in the spring of 1950, which might well have led to a substantial enlargement of the American military effort even if the Korean War had not intervened.

Against the background of Stalin's and Mao's military adventures in Korea, the concept of a possible Soviet timetable of military expansion spread; and this notion, quite different from the vision of the Soviet Union incorporated in the original containment doctrine, persisted down to the time when it became clear that both the Soviet Union and Communist China were prepared for a Korean truce.

In the interval that followed—roughly from June 1951 to March 1953—a fresh assessment of Soviet society and its future was made both within and outside the government. That assessment benefited greatly from the gradual fruition of the analyses, based in part on interviews with Soviet defectors in Germany, conducted by the emerging younger generation of American experts on the Soviet Union. These men, trained in the fields of sociology, psychology, anthropology, and economics, united what could be learned from books and documents with what could be learned from carefully structured interviews with former Soviet citizens. The conclusions fitted, in general, both the less formal perceptions of Kennan and Bohlen and the insights of the best older scholars. They permitted, however, a more systematic and complete picture of how a modern bureaucratic society had emerged in the Soviet Union out of the dynamics of the prewar Five-Year Plans, the Second World War experience, and the postwar Soviet efforts at reconstruction and expansion of external power. Specifically, they confirmed the likelihood that the Soviet Union was not operating on a fixed timetable for the achievement of world domination but was engaged in a systematic effort to maximize its external power within the limits imposed by the need to cope with its internal problems, on the one hand, and with the resistance met in the external world, on the other.

In the year or so preceding Stalin's death, there were widespread efforts to achieve a new vision of where Soviet society was headed and what influence the removal of Stalin was likely to have. There was obviously a problem for both social scientists and policy makers in speculating on the relationship between a massive bureaucratic structure, with evident momentum of its own, and the extraordinary concentrated power of one ruthless man. What would his withdrawal from the system mean? Those professionally concerned with this issue disagreed significantly in their predictions, as well as in the confidence with which they were prepared to predict, but there was virtually universal agreement that the Soviet Union as of the early 1950s was a complex societal structure in which there were many built-in resistances to radical change as well as some potentially explosive frictions. On the whole, the weight of professional analysis fell to the view that Stalin's death would release certain limited changes—backed by forces which the dictator had hitherto suppressed—without radically altering the contours of Soviet society or the content of the Soviet external objectives.

The effort to clarify the prospects for change in Soviet society interwove with an effort to develop more mature conceptions of what was then called psychological warfare. As the Cold War years rolled on, it became evident that some part in the conflict was being played by the American impact on the minds and attitudes of men and women in other societies, including Communist societies. When the Soviet Union acquired nuclear weapons, and the possibilities of a standoff in major weapons became more real, the psychological element in the struggle rose in priority.

Simultaneously, a technical problem arose when, in 1949–1950, the Soviet Union invested major resources in jamming American radio broadcasts to Russia and Eastern Europe. This crisis led to Project TROY, an analysis conducted at MIT of the technical, psychological, and political problems of communication from the United States to the Communist world. What emerged from Project TROY and the studies that succeeded it was a somewhat paradoxical conclusion: the American problem of communicating effectively was neither technical nor psychological in any narrow professional sense; the essential task was to project a clear, consistent image of U.S. purposes and policies that would match what, in fact, the nation did from day to day and that could be related to the lives and perspectives of other peoples. From this conclusion flowed few suggestions for new psychological tricks but, rather, the recommendation that the national government find better means for coordinating the flow of policy and action among the various arms, military and civil, which, in fact, dealt with the outside world. The problem of psychological warfare came to be conceived primarily as the task of making, executing, and articulating a coordinate policy that would dramatize the areas of overlap between the purposes of the United States and those of other nations. This was the approach adopted explicitly in 1953 by the committee headed by William Jackson to review policy in this area.

Thus, the Psychological Strategy Board, created in 1951, gave way, under the Eisenhower administration, to the Operations Coordinating Board, a useful committee at the undersecretary level that normally met over lunch on Thursdays, with a mandate, among other things, to render day-to-day operations mutually consistent and reinforcing. In addition, the role of special adviser to the president on the psychological impact of national policy was maintained during the Eisenhower first term.

Eisenhower evidently had other responsibilities in the period preceding his assumption of authority than to follow the development of a more mature image of the dynamics of Soviet society and a more mature conception of the nature and limits of psychological warfare. Nevertheless, three elements in his experience and policy converged to make him look toward the possibilities of change in Soviet society and toward a negotiation with the Soviet Union of a peace settlement.

First, like most Americans in the Control Council in Berlin in 1945 and 1946, Eisenhower had seen something of the generation of modern soldiers and technicians who had matured during the Five-Year Plans and the Second World War. While these men were obviously the instruments of Stalin's policy, they exhibited in human and professional interchange the existence of values and manners quite different from those of the dedicated professional international revolutionary; and they left among Americans, including Eisenhower, a sense that Soviet society might evolve in time into something different from what it appeared to be under Stalin—difficult but more livable in terms of American interests.

Second, this tempered optimism about the potentialities for change converged with Eisenhower's appreciation of the terrible destructiveness of the emerging new weapons. As with most professional soldiers, Eisenhower's understanding of the capabilities for destruction in nuclear weapons, compared with the weapons of the Second World War, made him regard a major war as not only irrational but almost unthinkable. While recognizing the need to deter the use of Soviet military force, he deeply believed that the nation would have to look to nonmilitary instruments to protect its interests, and this conclusion directly influenced his interest in psychological warfare.

Third, as noted earlier, the commitment of the new administration to seek a substantial reduction in defense outlays, combined with the drawing to a close of the Korean War, made it logical to conceive of a test of Moscow's purposes by the new administration.

Thus, it was natural that Eisenhower should not be reluctant to consider the possibility of negotiations with the Soviet Union centered about the question of the control of armaments.

4. Three Protagonists of Negotiation

This was the broad background against which Jackson, Kennan, and I came together in the wake of Stalin's death.

I was caught up in this process in a quite particular way. As the Korean War appeared to signal a new, intense, and protracted phase of the Cold War, extending far beyond Europe, it was decided to set up at MIT a Center for International Studies (CENIS). Its director, Max F. Millikan, a professor of economics, had done both wartime and postwar public service in Washington. He was also one of my oldest and closest friends, a tie reaching back to 1933–1934, when we learned our first economics, with two others, in an informal seminar. CENIS was created to bring to bear academic research on issues of public policy. It was financed by grants from both the government and private foundations. The fiscal agent for the government was the CIA, acting on behalf of the NSC community. The sort of policy-oriented research we planned to do—on Communist societies and the developing regions—would have better fitted the State Department, which had policy responsibilities, rather than the CIA, which did not; but the State Department lacked the funds for such enterprises. Private foundations supported wholly the CENIS work on development as well as a major study of American society in the late 1950s. The tie to the CIA in studies of Communist societies, however, proved congenial, and there was never the slightest effort by anyone in Washington to shape the conclusions we drew. Our major findings were published in conventional scholarly ways, and we gave the government such advice as we were moved by our studies to do.

As a social scientist without prior commitments in the field of Soviet affairs, I was asked, in 1951, to undertake an analysis of the dynamics of Soviet society while continuing my teaching of economic history. I put together a small research team, drew on all the learning and insights of academia and government, but made my own synthesis. The study (*The Dynamics of Soviet Society*) was turned in to the government in August 1952, published in 1953, with later editions in 1954 and 1967. We devoted a good deal of attention to what effects Stalin's death might have on Soviet domestic life and its foreign policy.

Our central perception arose from a triangular view of Soviet dispositions. In exercising power within the Soviet system, we viewed the rulers as confronted with the need to allocate their energies among three often competing objectives: the overriding requirement of managing high-level politics in ways which would maintain Communist party control over the country; the maintenance of minimum necessary popular support, including allocations to the production of consumer goods; and the extension of Soviet power abroad, including the buildup of potential military power at home. Over the span of Communist rule, a systematic pattern emerged among these objectives. When a crisis arose affecting one of them, pressure from the government eased in the other two directions. When, for example, Lenin found himself caught up in a serious challenge to his power with the Kronstadt revolt of 1920, he concentrated on consolidating his control over the Communist party but eased pressures on the people with his New Economic Policy and avoided external confrontations. Stalin behaved in a similar way while conducting his massive purges in the 1930s. It was a time when the constitution was promulgated, jazz, Christmas trees, and lipstick permitted, and a Popular Front policy conducted abroad. When the Germans attacked in 1941 and the security issue became overriding, Russian nationalism was evoked as the nation's binding cement, rather than Communist doctrine; and Stalin looked abroad for allies, nominally liquidating the Comintern.

On the basis of this recurrent pattern, we drew two major conclusions:

1. Since Stalin's death would constitute a major crisis in the organization of Soviet power, absorbing a great deal of attention among his possibly contentious heirs, its immediate aftermath was most unlikely to include Soviet adventures abroad.

2. If the American objective was to act in ways which maximized the chance of benign internal changes—an objective we commended—U.S. actions should not be threatening. External pressure was likely to force the Soviet leadership into a rigid unity unlikely to yield liberalization in domestic policy.

As for the possibilities of prompt major changes in Soviet foreign policy, our conclusions before the event were not highly optimistic.[14] We perceived Germany and arms control as the two central issues of the Cold War as of 1952. The argument was that a reversion of East Germany to democratic rule, as part of a unified nation under severe arms limitations, and acceptance of the mutual inspection required for serious arms control in general had implications for the stability of Communist domestic rule that rendered progress on these two central issues rather unlikely:

> It is, thus, our judgment that the ultimate obstacles to a diplomatic agreement on the decisive issues of the Cold War stem not from problems of Russian national security, but from the overriding priority of Soviet policy, namely, the maintenance of that regime's power over its Russian base. It follows, therefore, that a true liquidation of the Cold War— as opposed to a mitigation convenient, perhaps, for both sides—hinges on the possibility of change in the nature of

the Soviet regime, which would make its foreign policy a reflex of Russian national interest rather than the interest of a regime in perpetuating its own domestic power.[15]

Our bias, therefore, was for an American policy in the wake of Stalin's death which did what it could to encourage domestic changes toward a more liberal and nationalistic Soviet Union rather than one which looked with high expectations to a prompt and definitive resolution of the Cold War.

On the other hand, we felt that we had no right to be so confident in our conclusions as to rule out an effort to explore the possibility of radical change in Soviet external policy and that, if the exploration were properly conducted, it might provide a framework which would maximize the possibilities of liberalizing domestic change within the U.S.S.R.

This frame of reference, elaborated in some detail in *The Dynamics of Soviet Society*, explains the following suggestion from CENIS, passed to Washington on March 4, the day Stalin's illness was announced:

> Given the acute but temporary traumatic state of emotion in the Soviet Union and in the Communist bloc, we believe the government should consider a major Presidential initiative within the week made with Congressional backing if possible, along the following lines.
>
> 1. He should state that Stalin's death marks the end of an era and opens up fresh options for the Russian peoples. In particular it offers them a unique opportunity to remake their relations with the rest of the world;
>
> 2. The President should evoke the common wartime effort and the common wartime goals of the two nations for a peaceful, orderly world;
>
> 3. He should emphasize and illustrate in concrete terms that there is no incompatibility between American interests and objectives and the legitimate interests and objectives of the Russian nation and its peoples; and
>
> 4. He should announce his intention to initiate in concert with our allies a meeting in the near future designed to re-

examine the possibilities of agreement on controlled armaments, Germany, Austria, and other substantive issues in contention. There are, we believe, four reasons for such action:

(a) as a matter of historical record, the United States must not let this possibly brief period of unsettlement in the Russian outlook go by without holding up an image of our true intentions and purposes;

(b) such an initiative would solidify the Free World in its posture towards our future relations with the Soviet Union;

(c) such an initiative would help counter the fears of American aggression cultivated by Soviet propaganda and inevitably heightened by Stalin's removal from the scene. It would thus encourage those close to power who may be prepared to consider internal and external policies different from those of Stalin; and

(d) such an initiative would immediately confront the regime with a major policy decision of the first order of magnitude and help reveal its inner constitution and conflicts.

Evidently, these were propositions underpinning the draft I wrote two days later in Washington after discussion with Jackson.

It was not accidental that Jackson's and my views converged so promptly in response to Stalin's death. A graduate of Princeton, Jackson served on Eisenhower's staff in Africa and Western Europe in psychological warfare operations during the Second World War and emerged as an effective aide to Eisenhower during the 1952 campaign, after a professional career mainly with Time-Life-Fortune. While still attached to the Luce publishing empire, he was president of the National Committee for a Free Europe, an organization in support of freedom for the peoples of Eastern Europe which, among other things, had Radio Free Europe (RFE) under its wing. It was in this capacity that he called a conference at Princeton on May 10 to 11, 1952, where we first met.

Those present came from the State Department (including Charles Bohlen and former Ambassador Joseph C. Grew), RFE, the intelligence community (including Allen Dulles), plus a few academics. I was invited along because of my work in the CENIS project on Soviet society; my MIT colleague, Jerome Wiesner, was invited because of his work on Project TROY.

The purpose of the meeting was to explore the possibilities of solving a problem faced by RFE in broadcasting persuasively to Eastern Europe. RFE had developed considerable operational capabilities, but American policy offered an inadequate foundation for talking persuasively to Eastern Europeans in terms of their problems and aspirations. Clearly, the United States was not about to go to war with the Soviet Union to liberate Eastern Europe. The men and women living there had to go about the round of life within the closely inhibiting structure of the Communist states which had been consolidated over the previous seven years. What in U.S. purposes was relevant to their lives? What did we have to say?

Those representing RFE indicated that there was a fundamental lack of content in enunciated American policy on which persuasive and effective radio broadcasts could be based. The RFE position was supported by a number of those present, including myself. It was opposed by Bohlen, who felt that further statements of American policy would involve forward commitments which we might not be prepared to honor or which might embarrass the government at home and in its relations abroad with both allies and the Soviet Union. An important intervention was made by Grew, who expressed his profound regret that no effort was made to hold out before the Japanese people a vision of American intentions different from that projected in the Japanese press by the Japanese government in 1940 and 1941. At the close of the afternoon of May 11, a drafting committee was appointed to see if an agreed statement of American policy might be formulated which would better meet the requirements of RFE. A draft, presented and criticized at a morning meeting on May 12, was then further revised. The third draft produced by this meeting is included as Appendix G.

The papers and draft done at Princeton went to the government through Allen Dulles and Bohlen. There was some talk that the Princeton draft might be included in a high-level speech during the Truman administration but nothing came of it. During the summer, Jackson also sent Eisenhower the materials generated by the Princeton meeting and received a letter of August 22, 1952, reflecting Eisenhower's interest with a postscript: "Can I count on it that you people are now going to go ahead and develop an actual plan?" On leaving the group, on Saturday, May 12, Grew said that he somehow felt the meeting had been "historic." Looking back, there is a modest case for his view, for after a fashion it was a kind of first draft of Eisenhower's April 16, 1953, speech.

Jackson and I kept in touch after the May 1952 meeting, although he was caught up in the intense activity of the campaign. We met in November, after the election; but major exchanges of substance were initiated by our somewhat similar reactions to an interview with Stalin by James Reston, published on Christmas morning with some drama in the *New York Times* (see Appendix H). We agreed that Stalin's responses were essentially nonsubstantive and that sometime early in the new administration an initiative should be taken, independent of the Reston interview, to outline positively U.S. purposes in the world and to force a negotiation of the major outstanding issues: "disarmament, the unity of Germany, the gradual elimination of the Iron Curtain, Austria, Indo-China, and Korea." Against this background it is not difficult to understand why we worked easily and quickly together in the wake of Stalin's death.

The convergence of George Kennan's views with ours was, on the face of it, less likely, but he had fallen into a somewhat dissident position as containment unfolded under the leadership of Truman and Acheson.[16] The generalized phrases in his 1947 "X" article in *Foreign Affairs* might easily lend themselves to interpretation as including tight military containment of the Soviet Union. In fact, Walter Lippmann accused Kennan of holding precisely that view. But Kennan drew back from the arming of Germany and from a security pact with Japan. His instinctive judgment was that it was not necessary to confront the Soviet ground forces in Eastern Europe with a balancing counterforce, that Moscow would not attack even a thinly defended NATO area. He feared that Western force expansion, although undertaken for defensive purposes, would stir in Moscow fears of attack and generate a mood that all-out war with the West was inevitable. He also felt that, as a society, the United States was not capable of sustaining for the long pull a decisive military role in the European power balance. Here is Kennan's own description of his views and of his differences with his colleagues:

> Everyone else seemed content to accept the split of the continent as it then existed, to regard the possibility of its removal as too remote to constitute a factor in our calculations, and to conceive the future of Europe in terms of this existing situation. The Western Europeans were happy to have someone who would guarantee their security against both Russians and Germans and relieve them, in effect, of the necessity of having a policy of their own vis-à-vis either of those powers. . . . The Americans, on the other hand, already committed to a militarized view of the cold war, their policy already largely dominated by the conviction that the overriding consideration was to set up the military strength necessary to "deter" the Russians from attacking Western Europe . . . saw no reason to weaken this effort at military defense, just then finding its institutional form in NATO, by toying with plans which failed to include Britain, Canada, and the United States. . . .
>
> . . . My opponents, thinking in defensive terms, wished to see American military power held tightly at every point to the borders of the Soviet orbit—exactly the aberration of which Lippmann had accused me in 1947. I, in each case, wanted to hold the door open to permit the eventual emer-

gence of large areas (a united, demilitarized Germany, a united Europe, a demilitarized Japan) that would be in the military sense uncommitted, as between the two worlds. In each case, I was prepared to see us withdraw our military forces if Soviet power would be equivalently withdrawn and if we could look forward to the rise, in the areas thus thrown open, of political authority independent of Soviet domination. The new, independent Communist Yugoslavia suited my book perfectly, as did Sweden and the neutralized Austria. I would have liked to see this uncommitted area increased until it came to constitute a large part of the European continent. I believed that a readiness on our side to withdraw would eventually stimulate a disposition on the Soviet side to do likewise. Only in this way, as I saw it, could one bring about the withdrawal of the lines of Soviet power to limits more compatible with the stability of Europe and thus making a beginning, at least, at the correction of the great geopolitical disbalance to which the outcome of World War II had led.

This was the first objective I had in mind. But the second was to get us as soon as possible out of the position of abnormal political-military responsibility in Western Europe which the war had forced upon us. I had no confidence that a *status quo* dependent on so wide an American commitment could be an enduring one. Such bipolarity, I thought, might do for a few years; it could not endure indefinitely. . . . Some day, it appeared to me, this divided Europe, dominated by the military presences of ourselves and the Russians, would have to yield to something more natural—something that did more justice to the true strength and interests of the intermediate European peoples themselves. What was important was that our plans for the future should be laid in such a way as to permit that "something" to come into being when the time for it was ripe—not in such a way as to constitute an impediment to it.[17]

These views lay behind a paper formulated in the Policy Planning Staff during the Berlin blockade and submitted to Acheson on November 15, 1948.[18] It was a package of proposals for a general German settlement, known as Plan A. It involved the early creation of an all-German provisional government by free elections, as well as the mutual withdrawal of Western and Soviet forces from Germany except for garrison positions on the German periphery. Thus, from 1948 on, Kennan was prepared to contemplate a negotiation in which German democratic unity was traded for substantial demilitarization.

Jackson and I did not share Kennan's reasoning about NATO, and we believed a negotiation on German unity with Moscow would be more likely to succeed if the EDC had been agreed in principle—that is, prior agreement on EDC would constitute the most powerful bargaining chip available to the West in negotiating an all-German settlement with quite different security arrangements for Germany. But Jackson and I did share Kennan's view that existing dispositions in Western Europe were not an end in themselves and that we should be prepared radically to alter security arrangements in Europe if the Soviet Union were to agree to a Germany unified by free democratic elections. We also felt it was essential for the unity of the non-Communist world that the United States put forward, in good faith, credible proposals to this end, even if the odds on their acceptance appeared low. We felt that the split of Europe was dangerous as well as historically unnatural; that it could not be rationally resolved by war with the Soviet Union; that the human plight of the Eastern Europeans should not be callously accepted; and, therefore, that the effort should be made for peace in Europe consistent with Soviet as well as Western security interests and with expanded freedom for those who lived east of the Elbe. Kennan also took the view, at which we had arrived in *The Dynamics of Soviet Society*, that, in all probability, major changes in Soviet foreign policy were likely to emerge only as the result of slow but cumulative changes in the character of the Soviet system.

It is not difficult to understand, then, why Kennan, on the

afternoon of March 10, responded positively to a reading of our draft of Eisenhower's proposed statement.

As the chronological account in Appendix C indicates, Kennan arrived in Washington in the wake of Stalin's death by a kind of back door. On the night of March 5, Kennan happened to be in Cambridge and came to dinner at the home of Max Millikan, who gathered a group of friends, including, I believe, McGeorge Bundy, Kingman Brewster, and Elting Morison. Millikan and I were full of the ideas we had transmitted to the government the previous day. I was about to catch the night train to Washington, and we talked at length about what ought to be done. Kennan evoked eloquently, on his own, a case similar to that CENIS had just made for a major presidential initiative to explore the possibility of a more peaceful resolution of problems with the Soviet Union.

I felt it was somehow quite wrong for me, a newcomer to the field of Soviet studies, to be going to Washington at this critical juncture while Kennan, one of the few authentic experts the nation possessed, was not being consulted. On arrival, I raised the matter with Jackson. Without a moment's hesitation he ran down Kennan at his Pennsylvania farm and asked him to come to town. His exchanges with Jackson and me on the afternoon of March 10 are set out in Appendix C. Kennan saw, I believe, Allen Dulles, as well as Bohlen and other old friends, but the secretary of state did not receive him.[19]

As Jackson went into his NSC confrontation with the secretary of state the next day, I believe he felt a bit strengthened that at least one member of the Foreign Service was in support of his effort.

5. From March 11 to April 16, 1953

Eisenhower's April 16 speech emerged in the five weeks after the March 11 NSC meeting from the interplay of three tracks: the evolution of the Soviet peace offensive; the exchanges of view between the United States and its major allies; and the speech-drafting process which engaged the president and his staff, on the one hand, and Dulles and his staff, on the other.

The Soviet peace offensive began, in a small way, with a passage in Malenkov's funeral oration of March 10, including this sentence: "In the sphere of foreign policy, our principal concern is not to permit a new war, to live in peace with all countries." There was a good deal more in this vein, including ". . . a policy based on the Lenin-Stalin premise of the possibility of prolonged coexistence and peaceful competition of two different systems, capitalist and socialist." There was nothing remarkable in Malenkov's evocation of the peace theme. The language was familiar and, in the past, had proved consistent with some exceedingly unpleasant confrontations. And, indeed, rather sterile Soviet "peace offensives" had happened before. But, still, Malenkov's words were noted; and there was interest, even if skeptical interest, in what the words might come to mean, if anything.

The next move came six days later with the publication of Malenkov's brief but more operational statement to the Supreme Soviet: "At the present time there is no disputed or unresolved question that cannot be settled peacefully by mutual agreement of the interested countries. This applies to our relations with all states, including the United States of America."

The State Department immediately expressed "interest"; and, in a press conference of March 19, Eisenhower opened with a prepared statement including the following:

> . . . as you know, there has been an expression of an intent to seek peace, from the Kremlin. I can only say that that is just as welcome as it is sincere.
>
> There is a very direct relationship between the satisfaction of such a thing and the sincerity in which it is meant. They will never be met less than halfway, that I assure you; because the purpose of this administration will forever be to seek peace by every honorable and decent means, and we will do anything that will be promising towards that direction.

Some limited acts of substance followed Malenkov's statement published on March 16. On March 21, the Soviet government threw its weight behind a proposal, laid before the Korean negotiators by the United Nations commander in December 1951 and ignored for fifteen months, that ill and disabled prisoners of war be exchanged in Korea. On April 2, after the first positive Communist move in Korea, Eisenhower reinforced his positive pragmatic stance: ". . . we should take at face value every offer that is made to us, until it is proved not to be worthy of being so taken." There were, at this time, further indications that the truce stalemate at Panmunjom might be ending. At the other end of Eurasia, traffic tie-ups around Berlin were lifted and an atmosphere of quadripartite bonhomie regenerated. In New York the Soviet delegation at the United Nations agreed to Dag Hammarskjöld as secretary-general, ending a long impasse. As Philip Mosely was to point out later in the year in *Foreign Affairs*: "Some of the first steps in carrying out the new line were little more than gestures. . . . Some . . . have simply meant the scrapping of profit-less obstinacy. . . . The most striking shift in Soviet policy has been the conclusion of the Korean truce, the liquidation of one of Stalin's most glaring mistakes."[20] On Germany, there were vague suggestions, including one from the Soviet commander in Berlin that the negotiation of German unity might be possible.

All this was sufficient for the *New York Times* to observe as early as April 2 in an editorial that "since the death of Stalin an unmistakably softer wind has begun to blow out of Moscow and the various Communist moves are beginning to fall into a pattern which, if completed and validated, holds out the promise of at least a temporary easing of international tensions." And Eisenhower was prepared to acknowledge in his April 16 speech that "recent statements and gestures of Soviet leaders give some evidence that they may recognize this critical moment."

Soviet moves, gestures, and rhetoric, accompanied by some tentative relaxation of pressure on the Soviet peoples, were also sufficient to complicate diplomacy. Each of the leaders of the major allies in different ways faced the problem of responding to a public opinion which welcomed signs of an easing of tension with the Soviet Union. Their reactions are well summarized in Louis L. Gerson's account of their responses in April to a near final draft of Eisenhower's proposed speech:

> The President sent drafts of his speech to Churchill, Mayer, and Adenauer. He did not want to say anything publicly until he knew the allies were in agreement. He was anxious to have Churchill's reaction. All of the allied leaders thought the statement excellent, but only Adenauer gave unqualified support.
>
> The French Premier [who had ended a visit to the United States on April 2] applauded American initiative on the peace front and favored pressure on the Soviets to make agreements. He felt Soviet acceptance of an Austrian treaty followed by evacuation of troops from Austria, Hungary, and Rumania would give evidence of readiness to consider other

problems. Mayer opposed a summit conference, which pleased Dulles. The only comments of substance related to Germany and Indochina. The Premier feared a reunited Germany, which he assumed would be a neutral and disarmed Germany, before reaching an agreement with the Soviet Union. A reunited Germany might deal with the Soviet Union and Eastern Europe. France, he said, could not permit this unless with a simultaneous general disarmament. He supported EDC and rearmament of Germany as a means of convincing the Soviet Union of the desirability of general disarmament. The Premier requested the President to couple the demand for a Korean settlement with an end to the war in Indochina.

Churchill questioned some of the proposed address's assumptions. He felt that a change in Soviet mood and perhaps in policy had become apparent with the death of Stalin, and that the time was ready for informal, private conversation among a few leaders of the major powers. The Prime Minister doubted the wisdom of too many conditions as a means of testing Soviet intentions.[21]

Eisenhower's reply to Churchill "doubted the wisdom" of a summit meeting with the Russians but raised again the possibility of a gathering of the leaders of Britain, France, and the United States. As we shall see (pp. 62–63, below), Churchill was not that easily put off. As for the excessive conditions Churchill found in the draft, Eisenhower, using Churchill's language, replied on April 13: "I agree with the tenor of your comments and shall certainly strive to make my talk one that will not freeze the tender buds of sprouting decency, if indeed they are really coming out." Churchill's suggestion that the speech might be postponed until the Soviet stance was better defined was, after some uncertainty, set aside. There was even some suspicion in Eisenhower's entourage that Churchill hoped to make the first grand response of the West to the new situation in Moscow.

Adenauer had come to visit the United States after the passage of the EDC treaty by the Bundestag and was in Washington April 7 to 11. His assessment of the situation in the wake of Stalin's death and of the attitudes encountered in America are set down at length in his memoirs and captured in the following passage.

My visit to Washington took place during an extremely important period for American policy. It was at a time when the Soviet Union was starting a peace offensive. This peace offensive had produced a very insecure political situation. It seemed as though a large part of American public opinion was only too ready to succumb to the blandishments of a détente which for the time being was nothing but a pipe-dream. American families wanted their sons to come back from Korea. People were tired of war and its tensions. . . .

I was very interested to learn what the attitude of the United States was regarding the Soviet peace feelers that had been put out recently.

Eisenhower replied that America was endeavouring like any other people to preserve the peace. But as long as the Soviets wanted only a peace by force they must be stopped by force.

Secretary of State Dulles asked me whether I believed that the Russian peace feelers would have an effect on the attitude of the German people or on the EDC. . . .

I replied that Americans need have no fear that we in Germany might weaken. The Germans knew the Soviets and their totalitarian ways of thought better than most peoples. Also we knew from our experience during the National Socialist period how a totalitarian state conducts politics. America could rest assured that only a very few people in Germany would welcome a lessening in defence efforts on account of the Soviet peace feelers. . . .

Dulles asked me to describe my views on the Russian situation after the death of Stalin because he assumed that I had information the United States did not have.

I replied that . . . the Russian peace feelers were nothing but a sign that the new Soviet leaders needed a lull to settle their internal affairs and therefore wanted to ward off any disturbance that might impinge from outside. . . . There were no indications that Russia had desisted from her intentions. Rearmament was continuing unabated in the Soviet Union, especially along the Western front. . . .

. . . If the Soviet Union offered something concrete, one should accept it, but for the rest one should continue on the previous course and not be diverted from it. The Federal Republic certainly did not want war, but the danger of war would increase if the West relaxed its rearmament efforts. It would decrease if the West continued to rearm. . . .

On the reunification of Germany I said that this problem was not an isolated one, but a question closely and intimately linked with the question of Europe as such. A neutralized Germany was no solution. With the Soviet bloc on the one hand and on the other the free countries of Western Europe and far away the United States, and between them a neutralized Germany, the following development would probably take place: the influence of Soviet power and Soviet strength would be so great—it could be compared to a magnet which attracts iron—that after some time the Soviet Union would attract all the weakened European countries.[22]

Although Adenauer does not refer to prior knowledge of Eisenhower's speech, it is clear in a memorandum from Dulles to Emmet Hughes of April 10 (see Appendix I) that the speech was discussed and Adenauer had asked that a reference to German and Japanese prisoners of war still held in the Soviet Union be included. That reference was, indeed, added to the text. Four days earlier Dulles had recommended to Eisenhower that the language used with respect to Germany in the speech should be "checked with Adenauer," and this almost certainly was done. It is also likely that Adenauer welcomed Eisenhower's call for German unity for domestic political purposes. Later in the year, Adenauer was to press Dulles to initiate negotiations on German unity in order to assist him in the German general election of September 6 (see below, p. 65).[23]

Thus, Eisenhower was in a position to deliver his speech, having consulted in exemplary fashion and with his major allies more or less in support. In different ways each welcomed, for domestic reasons, the peaceful stance of the American leader; but they had quite different concerns and priorities, as the course of events in 1953–1954 was to reveal. Barring a Soviet willingness to accept German unity on something like Western terms, those differences were bound to assert themselves; and the French did not want German unity in any form, although they would have found it difficult to oppose if, in fact, it had been offered by Moscow in a form acceptable to Adenauer, Churchill, and Eisenhower.

The real problems in formulating the speech, however, lay in Washington, not abroad; and to evoke them we backtrack a month to the aftermath of Eisenhower's decisions at the NSC meeting of March 11 (see above, pp. 6–7).

As Appendix C indicates, there was the usual luncheon meeting of the Psychological Strategy Board (PSB) on Thursday, March 12, in the wake of the NSC session on the previous day. The group included Bedell Smith, Allen Dulles, and Jackson. There seemed unanimity that the government should move forward on the basis of the redrafted version of the proposed "Statement," and Smith promised to help with Foster Dulles.

But it was not all that easy. In the first place, what I had left behind with Jackson, as I returned to my teaching at MIT, was a rather austere draft of a possible presidential "Message to the Soviet Government and the Russian Peoples." It was initially designed for publication, not personal delivery. By the afternoon of March 12, it was envisaged that what the president had to say would be delivered either to the American people on television or to the U.N. General Assembly on Thursday, March 19. In addition, of course, despite apparent agreement in principle, there were bound to be differences of view about what, in fact, the president should say. All this resulted in a weekend of hard work, as the following memoranda of Dulles' telephone conversations indicate.[24]

March 13, 1953 [Friday]
TELEPHONE CONVERSATIONS WITH E. HUGHES
AND C. D. JACKSON

The Secretary spoke with Emmet Hughes about the draft speech for the President. Mr. Hughes has not done any work on it as yet, but is not happy with Jackson's draft. Neither is the Secretary happy with it and will see what he can do since Mr. Hughes does not want to get into any hassle over drafting. They exchanged ideas and decided that since they agreed they were wasting time talking to each other.

The Secretary then spoke with C. D. Jackson and agreed that it would be good for the three of them to meet Saturday morning here at 10 o'clock and see what they could work out.

March 16, 1953 [Monday]
MEMORANDUM OF CONVERSATION
WITH THE PRESIDENT

1. *Speech on Peace.* I told the President we had worked hard over the week end and now had a draft, which was being rewritten, and which I thought deserved his study. I told him that I thought it was even more essential that he make such a speech, in view of Malenkov's speech of yesterday. The President seemed disposed to move ahead, but said it was too bad that he had not made his speech before Malenkov.

March 16, 1953 [Monday]
TELEPHONE CONVERSATION WITH C. D. JACKSON

The Secretary telephoned to say that he had mentioned the speech to the President, who is looking forward to getting it and is disposed to go ahead if it fulfills his expectations. Jackson said he had done another draft, Hughes has another draft and will combine the two. When that is done he will send the Secretary a copy also.

This communal enterprise yielded four drafts, three dated March 16, one March 17, presumably the synthesis of the Hughes and Jackson drafts. All were geared to delivery before the U.N. General Assembly. Along the way it was evidently decided that the speech was not ready, and the notion of delivering it before the U.N. General Assembly was dropped. By March 21, Eisenhower was thinking of delivery on April 12 at the Pan-American Union.

In substance, what might be called the weekend drafts shifted the emphasis rather heavily to Eastern Europe, reflecting, no doubt, Jackson's concerns; and a format evolved counterposing what the United States sought in the world with the question: what is the Soviet Union prepared to do? The call for immediate negotiations with the Soviet Union on Germany had, of course, been dropped after the March 11 NSC meeting. I was shown one of these drafts while briefly in Washington during the week of the sixteenth and expressed the view that it was excessively negative. (See Appendix K, letter of April 1, 1953.) It was in response to one of these drafts that Eisenhower intervened rather dramatically in "mid March," according to Emmet Hughes' account:

> On this occasion . . . he grew more excited and intense. He began talking with the air of a man whose thoughts, after a permissive spell of meandering, were fast veering toward a conclusion. And—as always when he became intellectually stirred—he began to pace the oval room, in a wide arc around me. He spoke slowly, forcefully . . .
>
> "Look, I am tired—and I think everyone is tired—of just plain indictments of the Soviet regime. I think it would be wrong—in fact, asinine—for me to get up before the world now to make another one of those indictments. Instead, just *one* thing matters: what have *we* got to offer the world? What are *we* ready to do, to improve the chances of peace?
>
> "If we cannot say these things—A, B, C, D, E, F, G, just like that—then we really have nothing to give, except just another speech. For what? Malenkov isn't going to be frightened with speeches. What are we *trying* to achieve?"
>
> He stopped in his long, slow strides about the room, to punctuate his rhetorical question. I waited and watched the familiar features: the head martially high, the strong mouth

tight, the jaw set—and the blue eyes agleam and intent, staring through the tall windows to the long southern lawn, as if some distant tree secreted a response, or might nod encouragement, to his blunt inquiry.

He wheeled abruptly toward me and went on . . .

"*Here* is what I would like to say.

"The jet plane that roars over your head costs three-quarters of a million dollars. That is more money than a man earning ten thousand dollars every year is going to make in his lifetime. What world can afford this sort of thing for long? We are in an armaments race. Where will it lead us? At worst, to atomic warfare. At best, to robbing every people and nation on earth of the fruits of their own toil. . . .

"Now, there could be another road before us—the road of disarmament. What does this mean? It means for everybody in the world: bread, butter, clothes, homes, hospitals, schools—all the good and necessary things for decent living.

"So let *this* be the choice we offer. If we take this second road, all of us can produce more of these good things for life—and we, the United States, will help them still more. How do we go about it? Let us talk straight: *no* double talk, *no* sophisticated political formulas, *no* slick propaganda devices. Let us spell it out, whatever we really *offer* . . . withdrawal of troops here or there by both sides . . . United Nations–supervised free elections in another place . . . free and uncensored air-time for us to talk to the Russian people and for their leaders to talk to us . . . and concretely all that we would hope to do for the economic well-being of other countries.

"What do we say about the Soviet Government? I'd like to get up and say: I am *not* going to make an indictment of them. The past speaks for itself. I am interested in the future. Both their government and ours now have new men in them. The slate is clean. Now let us begin talking to each other. *And let us say what we've got to say so that every person on earth can understand it.* Here is what *we* propose. If you—the Soviet Union—can improve on it, we want to hear it.

"This is what I want to say. And if we don't really *have*

anything to *offer*, I'm not going to make a speech about it."

The excitement of the man and the moment was contagious and stirring.[25]

A Dulles memorandum of conversation with Emmet Hughes on March 16 suggests that was the day the Eisenhower-Hughes conversation occurred.

March 16, 1953
TELEPHONE CONVERSATION WITH EMMET HUGHES,
THE WHITE HOUSE

Mr. Hughes called the Secretary with reference to the draft speech for the President, and summarized the reaction of the President as follows:

"This is a fine speech as a speech but I still want to get to concrete proposals. The kind that are as specific as cutting armaments to 5%, getting armies out of this country or that country, free elections in this country or that country. If we are not prepared to do this, and we should be, then he doesn't think there is a speech to be made. He was quite emphatic about it, and quite eloquent."

Hughes suggested that they, as soon as the President had time, get together with the President and go over a list which Hughes will draw up of proposals, perhaps 20 of them, six or seven of which might be feasible.

The Secretary pointed out that it is pretty difficult to make concrete proposals, without checking them with our Allies. For instance, we could not take armies out of Austria or Germany without checking with the military people and with the French and English. Every one of the concrete things, as it approaches the area of reality, incurs serious difficulties with the Allies. He also mentioned that these were problems he should present to the President, not Hughes.

Hughes feels that it would save time in the long run if three or four of them could sit down with the President and the Secretary agreed to do this, Hughes will get up the list of suggestions.

He also brought out the fact that the President was strongly against using the UN, believing that it would invite more sterile debate there. The Secretary said that Malenkov's speech came about in a normal way and he had just added a few paragraphs aimed at us. The Secretary also mentioned the danger of getting into a corner on this willingness to meet with the Russian leader, there had been a response of a sort from Stalin to Reston and now Malenkov, it would be well to be sure we want to [do] this before we get trapped. Hughes will check the calendar and invite Jackson and Allen Dulles.

Mr. Hughes called back and said that 10:15 a.m. Tuesday, March 17 seemed to be the best time for the President. The Secretary agreed to rearrange his schedule.[26]

Hughes describes the meeting of March 17, when a good many specific ideas were canvassed, including a suggestion from Allen Dulles that the U.S. and the U.S.S.R. join in a program of economic assistance to Communist China.

The discussion on the seventeenth yielded a draft of March 19, which contained "America's Four Year Plan for Peace": arms expenditures not to exceed 10 percent of "national industrial product"; savings from arms reductions to go to a World Aid Fund; U.N.-inspected arms control; the peaceful use of atomic energy; "peace in Asia," including Indochina and Malaya as well as Korea; a "gradual lifting" of the Iron Curtain; unification of Germany and an Austrian peace treaty; withdrawal of U.S. and Soviet forces, and the forces of their allies, from "foreign soil."

In responding to the March 19 draft, Paul Nitze, head of the Policy Planning Staff, raised sharply again, in a memorandum to Dulles, some of the concerns he and his colleagues had felt from the beginning—notably, the slowing down of EDC and being forced into a negotiation with the Soviet Union (see Appendix D).

At this point there appears to have been a hiatus until a draft emerges on March 26 which includes, for the first time, the catalog of arms costs Eisenhower apparently ticked off ten days earlier. This was a period, in Hughes' account, when he and the president worked more or less regularly on their own. By March 26 the speech began to assume something more like its final form, although at least five further drafts lay ahead. The attack on Soviet policy in Eastern Europe was relatively cryptic; the emphasis shifted heavily to the burden of armament outlays and to arms control. In a reaction to the new draft's derating of Eastern Europe, Jackson sent a memorandum to Hughes on March 30 including this paragraph:

> I cannot re-emphasize too strongly the importance of the wording regarding the satellite countries. If their overall reaction to the speech is that despite brave platitudes regarding free elections, what we are really paving the way for is a sphere-of-influence peace between Russia and the U.S., it would strike a near-mortal blow to that whole area. And that is the area where the gravest problems to the new Soviet regime can be started. Therefore, that section I believe should be firmed up so that it is unmistakable that no matter what the overtones, or how great the willingness to sit down and discuss and negotiate, this must not be construed as an indication that we will sell these people down the river in the interests of a cold war truce between Russia and ourselves.[27]

At the beginning of April, the issues to be settled—aside from lingering reservations about whether the speech should be made at all—tended to come to rest around aspects of policy in Asia. In the end, as noted earlier, there were also modifications made in response to suggestions from Churchill, Mayer, and Adenauer when (around April 10) the draft was sufficiently crystallized to be presented to them for comment. In the final phase of the effort, Nitze and Hughes worked closely together despite the former's earlier reservations.

There were two related issues regarding the Far East:

1. On what terms should the United States settle for an end to hostilities in Korea?

2. What about the conflicts going on in Indochina and Ma-

laya and the latent conflict between the Chinese Communists and the Nationalists on Taiwan?

Dulles was evidently uneasy about a settlement in Korea which would merely recognize the status quo, including a Communist North Korea, with war continuing in Indochina. In a memorandum to Hughes of April 10 (see Appendix I) just before leaving on vacation, he noted that the references in the then current draft to "ending of wars in Asia gives me a little concern lest it commit us to end the Chinese Civil war and again to 'neutralize' Formosa." He had made a similar point in a memorandum of April 6 to the president, which made clear that part of his concern was with the domestic reaction (see Appendix F). He, no doubt, had in mind William F. Knowland and others in the Senate.

The final version of the speech included this passage in its definition of what "peace" required:

> The first great step along this way must be the conclusion of an honorable armistice in Korea.
>
> This means the immediate cessation of hostilities and the prompt initiation of political discussions leading to the holding of free elections in a united Korea.
>
> It should mean—no less importantly—an end to the direct and indirect attacks upon the security of Indo-China and Malaya. For any armistice in Korea that merely released aggressive armies to attack elsewhere would be fraud.

There was no reference whatsoever in the final text to Formosa or, indeed, to Communist China.

Thus, what had begun as a call for prompt negotiation with the Soviet Union on Germany and other outstanding issues, to be transmitted immediately in the wake of Stalin's death, became, six weeks later, an eloquent definition of the American vision of what peace required in Europe, Asia, and the control of arms, coming to rest on a question put to the new Soviet leaders: how far are you willing to go? A good deal of the bone structure of the statement proposed on March 6 survived the many subsequent drafts: the evocation of war-time alliance, the contrast between the U.S. and Soviet post-1945 concepts for achieving security, the dangers to all in existing dispositions, the opportunity the moment offered for a fresh start, the ending of hostilities in Korea as a precondition, the need for reduced armaments and the commitment of direct savings to assist developing countries, the need for an Austrian treaty, the requirement of ending the division of Germany and Europe, and the assertion that the U.S. and its allies would persist in their joint efforts until effective measures of collective security were agreed with the Soviet Union and put into effect. But, in the course of the exercise, Eisenhower had put his mark on the speech in several important ways: by setting aside an explicit call for negotiation, by strengthening and greatly elaborating the passages on the need for arms control, by resisting inflammatory language on the liberation of Eastern Europe, and by resisting elaborate preconditions for a Korean settlement on the thirty-eighth parallel. As delivered, it was an authentic expression of his vision of what a peaceful world community required, and it was a vision which an overwhelming majority of the American people were prepared to support. But, in itself, it set in motion no courses of action to move the world closer to that vision.

6. The Aftermath

Preparations by Jackson for the distribution of the speech had been thorough, and the immediate popular reaction to the speech at home and abroad was extraordinarily positive. On April 16, before the returns were in, Jackson, in a letter to Dulles, returned to the issue of negotiations with Moscow on which he and I (and Kennan) had fought and lost on March 11 (see Appendix L). After noting that the burden of implementing the president's speech would fall with greatest weight on diplomacy and the secretary of state, he raised the possibility again of U.S. initiation of a four-power conference; urged, in any case, advance planning for such a conference; and underlined the virtue of persuading the Western European allies that the optimum stance for a four-power meeting was with EDC ratification complete. Dulles' response on April 21 was confined to the statement that advance planning was necessary and under way.

The government as a whole, however, was not so sharply focused on what the next steps should or should not be. When the cabinet met in Eisenhower's absence under Nixon's chairmanship on April 17, the talk was all of domestic politics and budgets; there was no reference to the president's initiative. Hughes wrote in his diary: "I suppose a lot of people thought we spent this day in the White House talking about the peace of the world."[28]

On the eighteenth Dulles addressed the American Society

of Newspaper Editors (see Appendix E). He argued that Eisenhower's words, which could have been spoken "at any time during these past ninety days, . . . gained immensely in significance because they come against a background of cohesive, positive action." He then marched through his agenda as he saw it: EDC and NATO, the role of the Seventh Fleet in protecting Formosa but not the Chinese mainland, aid to the French in Indochina, a tightening of the blockade of the Chinese mainland, the Captive Nations Resolution before Congress. He described the recent Soviet moves as "peace *defensive*," responding to the strength of U.S. policy. He called on Moscow to meet "the Eisenhower tests" and to "abolish and abandon, in fact as well as in name, the Cominform." It was pretty much a business as usual Cold War speech. And this was noted in a *Pravda* commentary on April 25 (see Appendix M), when the full text of Eisenhower's talk was published. Referring to Dulles' "belligerence," *Pravda* concluded that "if the real meaning of Eisenhower's statement is what was represented in Dulles' more detailed speech, delivered after the President's, before the same audience and in the same hall, it cannot produce positive results from the point of view of the interests of strengthening peace."

With respect to Eisenhower's text, *Pravda* provided a long, temperate but firm reply, point by point. (Appendix M also reproduces Bohlen's analysis of the *Pravda* statement, sent to Washington on April 25.) It resisted the notion of preconditions and special requirements which the Soviet Union had to meet, suggesting that the responsibility for moving forward was joint and that Moscow was ready for "a serious, businesslike discussion of problems both by direct negotiations and, when necessary, within the framework of the U.N."

Then, on May 11 and 12, the British spoke out: first Churchill acting as foreign secretary, with Anthony Eden ill, as well as prime minister; then Clement Attlee as leader of the opposition (see Appendix N). Churchill returned to the theme of his earlier exchanges with Eisenhower:

It would, I think, be a mistake to assume that nothing can be settled with Soviet Russia unless or until everything is settled. A settlement of two or three of our difficulties would be an important gain to every peace-loving country. For instance, peace in Korea, the conclusion of an Austrian Treaty—these might lead to an easement in our relations for the next few years, which might in itself open new prospects to the security and prosperity of all nations and every continent. . . .

I must make it plain that, in spite of all the uncertainties and confusion in which world affairs are plunged, I believe that a conference on the highest level should take place between the leading Powers without long delay. This conference should not be overhung by a ponderous or rigid agenda, or led into mazes and jungles of technical details, zealously contested by hordes of experts and officials drawn up in vast, cumbrous array. The conference should be confined to the smallest number of Powers and persons possible. It should meet with a measure of informality and a still greater measure of privacy and seclusion. It might well be that no hard-faced agreements would be reached, but there might be a general feeling among those gathered together that they might do something better than tear the human race, including themselves, into bits. . . .

I only say that this might happen, and I do not see why anyone should be frightened at having a try for it. If there is not at the summit of the nations the will to win the greatest prize and the greatest honour ever offered to mankind, doom-laden responsibility will fall upon those who now possess the power to decide. At the worst the participants in the meeting would have established more intimate contacts. At the best we might have a generation of peace.[29]

Attlee was a bit more pointed in his criticism of the Eisenhower administration's dual stance:

It is worth while saying a few words about the United States and about American policy. I hope they will cause no offense. I hope that no one will suggest that I am in any way anti-American. . . .

The Prime Minister comes to the House and states his policy. It is the policy of the Government. He can, if he wishes, get a vote in this House in support of it or he can, as in this debate, be satisfied with the great measure of support on both sides. That policy is Government policy and will be carried out by Ministers and by officials. Look on the other side. President Eisenhower makes a great speech. . . . shortly thereafter the Secretary of State Mr. Dulles makes a speech, which, I thought, struck rather a different note. We do find on occasions that there is one policy being run by the Treasury, another by the State Department, and perhaps another by the Pentagon.

Eisenhower and Dulles were not pleased with Churchill's intervention, and Harold Macmillan and Eden thought the proposed summit meeting with Moscow might be premature.[30] In much the mood of Dulles and Adenauer, Eden doubted "whether the policy of sustained pressure on Russia and the building up of strength in Europe had yet gone far enough to permit of such an attempt at détente." But Churchill, brooding about the probable early emergence of Soviet as well as American fusion weapons, with all they implied for the character of a major war between the great powers, felt the moment had to be seized and direct conversations undertaken with Moscow at the highest level.

It was clearly time for the West to align its policies toward Moscow. Eisenhower's March 11 suggestion of a possible Big Three summit meeting (see above, p. 7) was adopted and scheduled for Bermuda on June 17. The meeting was first delayed by a prolonged interregnum in the French government, as Mayer fell and a month passed before Joseph Laniel was found as an acceptable successor on June 26. The next day Churchill's inability to go to Bermuda was announced. He had suffered a stroke on June 23.

The aftermath of Stalin's death also generated two dramatic events in the East: the June riots in East Germany, which began on the night of June 16, after some six weeks of movement toward liberalization; and, in early July, the arrest of Beria, possibly connected with the East German uprising (see below, p. 71). Beria's arrest occurred just as the three Western foreign ministers were meeting in Washington in lieu of the Bermuda summit. It was at these sessions, which ended on July 14, that it became apparent that a conference on Germany with the Soviet Union was required: Bidault, then French foreign minister, made it clear to Dulles that the French parliament would not pass EDC unless a good-faith effort to solve the German problem by negotiation with the Soviet Union had been made and had failed; and, despite his skepticism regarding the outcome, Adenauer sent a message to Dulles asking for the announcement of a four-power meeting on Germany to assist him in the general elections of September 6. Thus, by mid July 1953, some four months after Stalin's death, the allies offered to negotiate about Germany with Moscow; and they did so not because the signals from Moscow were more propitious than they had been earlier but because the enterprises of the alliance could not move forward until the Soviet position on Germany had been tested.

After a "dreary interchange" of diplomatic notes in the autumn, to use Macmillan's characterization, the four foreign ministers, meeting in Berlin, finally came to grips with the German question in January 1954. By that time the Soviet Union had weathered tolerably well the East German revolt, had exploded a hydrogen bomb on August 20, and had decided it was prepared to make no concessions whatsoever on Germany. The Western powers were well prepared for the Berlin sessions, strengthened by the holding, at last, of a summit meeting in Bermuda in December 1953. The meeting generated no new propositions but permitted the foreign ministers, with support from their principals, to consolidate their positions before heading for Berlin and the long-delayed confrontation with Molotov. Before they arrived, Eisenhower had launched on December 8 his "Atoms for Peace" proposal at the United Nations General Assembly and, two weeks later,

Dulles had evoked his "agonizing reappraisal" threat; that is, the United States might have to consider withdrawing its troops from Europe unless the French parliament accepted the EDC.

Whether this possibility affected Soviet dispositions in Berlin we do not know. It is clear that Molotov was under instructions to give no ground on Germany or, indeed, on anything else. A detailed account of how the conference unfolded from the first formal session on January 25 to its dismal closing on February 19 is not relevant to this essay.[31] Three points are, however, worth noting:

1. By agreement, Eden took the lead in elaborating the Western proposal with its five-point sequence: free elections throughout Germany, a national assembly resulting from the elections, drafting of a constitution, formation of an all-German government responsible for negotiating a peace treaty, and signature and entering into force of the peace treaty. The new government would have the authority to assume *or reject* (a Dulles emendation) rights or obligations previously assumed by the federal government or Soviet Zone of Germany. The Western foreign ministers argued that the EDC, limiting the German army to twelve divisions, would constitute a useful arms limitation measure for the interests of Britain, France, and Benelux, wholly converged with the Soviet interest in preventing a full resurgence of German military power.

2. Molotov argued that a German government should be first set up by the occupying powers, incorporating the existing two regimes; that parliamentary democracy was inappropriate; and that Germany should have a national army. Above all, he argued that EDC should be abandoned, NATO disbanded.

3. On February 10 Molotov held up a vision of a Western Europe associated with the Soviet Union, via a European Security Pact—a Europe detached from the United States, which, along with China, would be an "observer." (Appendix

O gives C. D. Jackson's vivid account of the day as well as Eden's more austere appraisal.)

Whether Molotov was trying to encourage Britain and France to accept an "agonizing reappraisal" by the United States or simply overplayed his hand is not clear. But Dulles handled well this and other aspects of the conference;[32] and Molotov's position left no doubt in the minds of the Western governments that, as of early 1954, there was no realistic possibility for negotiating German unity or avoiding the absorption of the Federal Republic into the enterprises of the West as a full partner.

But this did not happen through the EDC. The French assembly rejected the EDC on August 30, 1954, by a vote of 319 to 264. At British suggestion, the Federal Republic was invited to join a Western European Union (WEU) superseding the Brussels Pact of 1948. This looser organization, with full British membership, filled the gap left by the failure of the EDC. The French retained their national army and had the British at their side. Thus, the occupation of the Federal Republic ended on October 23, 1954, with the formal signing of the WEU agreement and its entrance into NATO.

The major operational result of the Berlin conference arose from the powerful pressures in French political life to negotiate some kind of Indochina settlement. It yielded agreement to hold a further foreign ministers meeting in Geneva on unresolved Asian problems in which Communist China would participate. That protracted conference (April 26 to July 21) finally produced the armistice in Indochina at the seventeenth parallel with Communist control of the north. A few years of relative peace descended on that bedeviled region, the only such interval experienced from 1946 to 1981. In 1955, the negotiations on the Austrian State Treaty were completed and that country assumed fully its place in the international community. And, in general, the period from Stalin's death to, say, the nationalization of the Suez Canal by Nasser on July 26, 1956, was the least troubled period in the protracted struggle between the Soviet Union and the West that followed the Second World War. When a period of acute tension resumed, its regional focus shifted from Europe and Korea to the Middle East, Africa, and Latin America, although the struggle in Southeast Asia revived in 1958; and the new phase of confrontation was framed by the arms race in missiles, tipped with fusion weapons, which were rapidly developed on both sides during the somewhat illusory quiet of the three years that followed Stalin's death.

7. Some Conclusions

In terms of ideas and action, the U.S. government's decisions, from Stalin's death to Eisenhower's April 16 speech, constitute the resolution of a series of clashes. Among them was Eisenhower's instinct to speak out promptly versus Dulles' reserve; between those, including Churchill, who felt that high-level diplomatic contact with the Russians should be sought at Western initiative, versus those, including Eisenhower, who drew back from summitry in particular, quadripartite negotiation in general; between those who judged that the democratic unification of Germany, and the ending of military confrontation in the center of Europe, justified the exploration of radically new security dispositions versus those who either felt German unity was undesirable on any terms (the French) or were prepared to pursue it only on the basis of the further consolidation of the Western security position along familiar lines (Adenauer); between those who felt that Soviet policy would be determined on grounds quite independent of what the United States and the West did versus those who felt that there was a margin of Western influence on Soviet dispositions and that it should be exercised. Then there were elements of personality—notably, Eisenhower, Dulles, and the relationship between them. And, as always, there was politics—notably, the shadow of the Republican right wing, including not only Knowland and Taft but also McCarthy, still gathering momentum in the Senate.

Out of this mélange came five weeks of delay, a benign and successful speech, and a sterile negotiation at the foreign minister level nine months later forced on the United States by the domestic political requirements of the French and German governments.

The first question to pose is, was anything lost by this outcome? Was an opportunity forgone when Eisenhower turned down Churchill's suggestion for a prompt summit meeting and backed Dulles against Jackson in the NSC meeting of March 11?

One of the most interesting judgments on this matter is the retrospective view of Charles Bohlen, incorporated in his June 1964 Dulles oral history interview:

> . . . looking back on it, there are a number of things that might have been done, and I think that one of them might have been to have gone along with Winston Churchill's appeal in the spring of '53 for a Summit conference. . . . And from what we know now, this would have been a very fruitful period and might easily have led to a radical solution in our favor of the German question—because subsequent to that in '54—or later on in '53—there were a number of rumors around Moscow that the Russians had been thinking of the possibility of giving up East Germany. A year or so ago, Khrushchev made the same charge against Malenkov and Beria. But I think this was a mistake. I think it would have been very useful to have had a Summit conference in '53. We might have gotten a great deal out of it. I must say, I didn't advise it then, because I didn't see the situation as it looks now.[33]

Richard Goold-Adams reports, without providing his source, a similar retrospective view of Foster Dulles:

> By the time that January, 1954, arrived Dulles felt that the chances of reaching any significant agreement with the Russians, never more than slim, had grown even slimmer. He was inclined to think that, if a conference had been possible immediately after Stalin's death, or if the famous riots in East

Berlin had never taken place, the chances of a breakthrough would have been better. But, with the passage of time, the psychological elements in the situation were hardening as it was inevitable that they would in a period when the realities of nuclear power were so patently shifting.[34]

Of all the possible reasons for regret over the delay in negotiations with the Soviet Union, the most interesting—even tantalizing—centers on the course of Soviet policy in East Germany from, say, early May to the riots which began on the evening of June 16.[35] Evidently under Soviet pressure, the German Communist leaders undertook a wide-ranging set of moves which appeared, at least, to liberalize marginally life in East Germany. It was announced that consumer goods production would be increased; controls over labor were somewhat relaxed; farmers were reassured that they would not be forced into collectives; amiable gestures were made toward the German clergy and even non-Communist politicians; criticisms of the FRG were somewhat muted.

It seems reasonably clear from a variety of sources, including several East German Communist defectors, that Wilhelm Zaisser, minister of state security in East Germany, was associated with this policy, and that his sponsor was Beria. A decade later, in March 1963, Khrushchev, in fact, accused Beria of having plotted with Malenkov to liquidate East Germany as a Communist state in a negotiation with the West. Those who accept something like this interpretation argue that the liberalization was designed to render East Germany a more respectable negotiating partner in an all-German settlement. Even before later evidence developed, the rather hard-minded Philip Mosely presented something approximating this assessment in his *Foreign Affairs* article of October 1953. And it may be that, when Churchill spoke in the House of Commons on May 11, he had not only observed what was beginning to happen in East Germany but had in hand some intriguing intelligence. Others have remained skeptical that the limited liberalizing moves in East Germany had any such grand purpose.

In any case, the possibility—such as it may or may not have been—disappeared with the East German riots in June, the intervention of Soviet forces, and the reconsolidation of a hard-line Communist dictatorship in East Germany. The whole episode, however, with its vivid demonstration of the feelings of the East Germans, heightened the issue of German unity in the West German elections, helping lead Adenauer to advocate an early Western negotiation on the subject with the Soviet Union.

In the ten months between Stalin's death and the opening of the Berlin talks, five things had happened, then, that bear on Bohlen's and Dulles' second thoughts: there was time for the new men in Moscow to get over the shock and, after eliminating Beria, to settle into an uneasy collective leadership; there were the East German riots in June and the successful reconsolidation of Communist power after the intervention of elements from more than twenty Soviet divisions; the first Soviet fusion weapon was exploded in August; Moscow was able to observe the acute difficulty confronted by the French government in mobilizing parliamentary support for EDC, leading Dulles to evoke his "agonizing reappraisal"; and there was a substantial reduction in the American military budget. Taken altogether, it is not difficult to understand that the Soviet government judged, as of January 1954, that it could afford to stand pat on Germany, observe what transpired with the EDC, and see whether, in fact, the U.S. might reduce or withdraw its military commitment from Western Europe. From Roosevelt's statement at Yalta that U.S. forces could not be maintained in Germany for more than two years down to the present, the possibility of American detachment from Europe has been a recurrent Soviet hope, explicitly evoked, for example, at the Berlin conference in February 1954, at the Geneva summit of July 1955, in the Kennedy-Khrushchev exchange in Vienna in June 1961, and most recently in Georgi Arbatov's authoritative article published in the United States in April 1980.[36]

There is no solid evidence that Moscow would have been prepared in the spring of 1953 or in the immediate aftermath of the East German revolt of June to have contemplated a radical change in German policy; but it does seem likely that the chances for a substantial alteration in the contours of the Cold War would have been higher at a summit meeting in, say, April or May 1953 than at a foreign ministers meeting in early 1954. There may have been an interval of fluidity, although the evidence for it is limited and inconclusive, but at the Berlin foreign ministers conference all hands were pretty much back in the old ruts.

What, then, explains Eisenhower's curious position: he clearly felt there was a historic moment to be exploited, but he drew back from a meeting with the Russians at his initiative. He regretted that he had, in effect, been prevented by Dulles from preempting Malenkov in the launching of a post-Stalin peace offensive; but, in his April 16 speech, he left it wholly up to Moscow to propose or not to propose diplomatic courses of action. From the beginning, the State Department, as well as Jackson, perceived that serious progress on Germany, Austria, arms control, and the other issues placed on the agenda by the president could occur only in the context of negotiation. Why did Eisenhower resist?

In broad terms, Eisenhower addresses himself at some length in his memoirs to the question of summitry.[37] He reviews the disappointing experiences of Wilson and Franklin Roosevelt and describes his general attitude toward such meetings in these terms: ". . . I was still not willing to meet with Communist leaders unless there was some likelihood that the confrontation could produce results acceptable to the peoples of the West." On the post-Stalin period, he notes Dulles' opposition to a summit, Churchill's advocacy, Eden's reservations, and continued press discussion. He concludes:

At home and abroad the subject continued a live one. The constant debate—pro and con—assured the persistent interest of the press; so I developed a stock answer to any question about a possible Summit. I would not go to a Summit merely because of friendly words and plausible promises by the men in the Kremlin; actual deeds giving some indication of a Communist readiness to negotiate constructively will have to be produced before I would agree to such a meeting.

There is no reason to doubt that Eisenhower faithfully recorded the basic reasons for his reserve.

But I suspect three other elements converged to help produce his stance on this matter. First, summit meetings with Russians were not in good repute in Republican circles as of early 1953. There had been a good deal of Republican talk during the campaign about the alleged failure of Yalta and Potsdam. Here the shadow of the Republican right wing may have mattered. Eisenhower did not wish, I suspect, to begin his period of responsibility with a meeting of uncertain outcome in which he would be a central figure.[38] Thus, he turned off Churchill's proposals on March 11 and again on April 13, with the possibility of a politically safer Western summit.

Second, Eisenhower did not regard himself as a professional diplomatic negotiator. He had a clear picture of what leadership at his level demanded: setting a broad course for the nation and the world, administering the executive branch and its relations with Congress in a way that maintained reasonable consensus and courses of action that did not grossly violate the general directions in which he proposed to move. But, quite unlike Churchill, Eisenhower did not regard himself as both policy maker and operator. He had risen in the military as an officer of the staff rather than the line. He came to the top of his profession, through no fault of his own, without a field command. He was as successful as a man could be as an executive organizing and managing others in large enterprises. He did not shirk tough decisions in what he regarded as his proper domain. He was a natural and accomplished politician. Without question he rather than Dulles made the basic foreign policy decisions of his administration. But, both in military and political life, he drew back from imposing on his subordinates his concept of how operations should be conducted in detail. In the wake of Stalin's death, he lacked Churchill's confident eagerness, despite his seventy-eight years and gathering infirmities, to come directly to grips with the new Soviet leadership and assess what could or could not be wrung from the new situation.

Third, there was John Foster Dulles. Eisenhower accepted Dulles as a skilled professional in diplomacy. He had chosen him, was pleased with his choice, and was determined to work with him.[39] But at this juncture Eisenhower could not achieve with Dulles the common vision and common conception of the course of action to be followed that Kennan correctly defined as the necessary and sufficient condition for implementing the draft "Statement" Jackson showed Kennan on March 10. Not for the last time during his tenure as president, Eisenhower acted at his level as his instincts told him to act, but he did not insist on the operational follow-through implicit in the rhetorical position he took.[40]

Thus, Eisenhower reached out and spoke on April 16 with evident sincerity about peace. In phrases he used on another occasion, he aimed "to attack the future" rather than "worry about the past."[41] As a professional soldier, he knew better than most that, in a world where fusion weapons would be in the hands of both the Soviet Union and the United States, a military resolution of the conflict between the two countries was irrational. Describing Eisenhower's view of political warfare in a letter to me of December 31, 1952, Jackson wrote that he "appreciates that practically every other golf club in his bag is broken. . . ." Abstracting from the vocabulary of the day, Eisenhower was trying to use his position and his personality to nudge the world toward peace. As he said to his aide Andrew Goodpaster in 1956: "Of course we have got to have a concern and respect for fact and reiteration of official position, but we are likewise trying to 'seek friends and influence people.'"[42] But, lacking a secretary of state who shared his view of what was required and being uncertain about the appropriate diplomatic course to be followed, he settled for a good speech.

A word should be said here about C. D. Jackson and his role in this affair. Aside from Churchill, he was the only man in direct communication with Eisenhower who argued that negotiations should be promptly initiated by the West with the Soviet Union. His work with RFE and his very considerable knowledge of both Western and Communist Europe had led him to believe that a more positive image of U.S. purposes needed to be articulated and projected and that it was the American interest and duty to try to undo the split of Europe. His instinct told him that Stalin's death was a moment to try and that time might be short.

In a new administration, where his status as a White House aide was inherently uncertain and ill defined, Jackson exhibited rare courage: he brought Kennan, then regarded by Dulles (as well as Moscow) as something of a pariah, to Washington for consultation; with knowledge of State Department opposition, he laid before the NSC meeting of March 11 the papers we had generated; and he argued his case head-on against the secretary of state. Moreover, he did not hesitate to come back to urge prompt negotiations in a letter to Dulles immediately after Eisenhower's April 16 speech. He did these things without generating personal hostility from Dulles or weakening his status with Eisenhower. Jackson proved able to sustain this pattern of strong advocacy of unorthodox or dissident positions, within the framework of amity with Eisenhower and Dulles, both as a working member of the administration (down through March 1954) and, subsequently, as a frequent consultant. As Nelson Rockefeller's experience in 1954 and 1955 was to reveal, this was not easy to do. (Rockefeller's vicissitudes constitute one of the strands in the next book of this series.)

Jackson's ability to carry off this bureaucratic tour de force hinged on a number of factors: his personal tie to Eisenhower, reaching back to Algiers in 1942 and his significant role in Eisenhower's 1952 election campaign; Eisenhower's bringing him on to his staff as a man to generate new policy concepts, a role that inherently carried a fairly wide bureaucratic license; and his base in the Luce empire, to which it was known he intended to return. Jackson clearly had no bureaucratic or political ambitions and was judged correctly in Washington to be immune from Potomac fever. His ties to the Luce publications made him a man high political figures would prefer not to offend. But there were also two rather special aspects of his personality that contributed to his capacity to crusade in dead seriousness in a setting of amiability. First, he brought to his relations with Eisenhower and Dulles an authentic affection and, even, a compassion for the responsibilities they carried. As will emerge in the next two books in this series, this human empathy permitted Dulles to confide in Jackson on several occasions in a rather extraordinary way. (One example is reflected on pp. 80–81, below.) And he did not hesitate to put his views before Eisenhower with a bluntness presidents rarely hear, confident that, if he triggered a passage of red-necked temper, it would quickly pass.

Second, there was Jackson's rather deceptive personal style. This tall, vigorous figure in his fifties had about him a boyish exuberance. In small talk his vocabulary smacked more of journalism and advertising than politics and diplomacy. He was systematically unpompous, humorous, and a companion to be enjoyed. But, when he settled down to a job of work, he could be thoroughly professional—comfortable and firm in loyalty to his own values and insights and his large vision of what the United States should stand for on the world scene. It was easy to underestimate Jackson, as a good many men in the Washington bureaucracy did; and, in a curious way, this was an asset.[43]

Dulles is generally portrayed in this passage as the hard-hearted cold warrior, resisting and then diluting the decent and generous impulses of his chief, arguing also against summitry both in March, in Washington, and in October 1953 when he met with Churchill in London. But, as suggested earlier (pp. 15–16, above), his problem as secretary of state was real, not merely the product of a rigid Presbyterian crusade against the evil he perceived in Communism. He correctly judged the chances of a Soviet change of heart on Germany to be slight—that is, of an agreement on German unity consonant with Western interests. And this skepticism was shared in the foreign offices of London, Paris, and Bonn with which he dealt. He inherited the mission of strengthening the West with a substantial military contribution from Germany in ways which would restore German sovereignty on terms acceptable to the other states of Western Europe. The task was extremely difficult, notably in France. The EDC was by no means assured. Dulles' reaction to Jackson's draft "Statement" was, simply, that its issuance would gravely endanger this major, fragile Western enterprise in mid passage; and, even when the call for negotiation was removed, after the March 11 NSC meeting, the president's speech still, he thought, carried with it that danger which, however, he came to regard as inevitable once Malenkov launched Moscow's peace offensive. As one who differed with Dulles at the time and would differ still, in retrospect, I believe he must be accorded the kind of acknowledgment Kennan made to Acheson's 1948 opposition to the Planning Staff's Plan A for a united Germany (see above, pp. 42–44):

> I was far then, and am far today, from being without sympathy for Mr. Acheson's position. The responsibility that rested on him was great. For him, too, the London Program, adopted and put in hand long before he became Secretary of State, represented a species of *fait accompli*. It could not be

lightly placed in jeopardy. He had a solemn duty to preserve Western unity, to carry forward the improvement and consolidation of political and economic conditions in Western Germany, to avoid things that could unduly excite the ready suspicions and anxieties of our Western European Allies. No immediate Russian agreement could have been expected at that time to proposals along the lines of Plan A. The imprudent advancement of them, on the other hand, could easily alarm and disorient Western opinion. To ask him to toy with such proposals was, in the circumstances, asking a great deal.[44]

Dulles' failure, in my view, lay not in his skepticism that the German issue could be solved in 1953 by negotiation with Moscow but in certain quite specific and narrow professional errors: his gross overstatement at the March 11 NSC meeting of the consequences of the president's proceeding with the proposed "Statement" (that is, the French and German governments would fall in a week, etc.); his failure to find a formula—or even to seek a formula—which might have persuaded the European allies that a negotiation on Germany had a much greater chance of success if EDC were, in principle, agreed than if its fate were still moot when the negotiation took place; his failure to anticipate the possibility of a Soviet peace offensive and thus the reluctant, defensive posture in which he found himself from Malenkov's statement published on March 16 forward, a posture which may have been costly because it was quite apparent to Moscow and may well have colored their dispositions at the Berlin conference of January and February 1954; his failure to sense at the time that the softening of Soviet policy in East Germany might conceivably represent an opening for serious diplomacy on a German settlement; and his apparent failure to take into account the possible effects in Moscow of his threat to Western Europe of an American "agonizing reappraisal," if EDC were not consummated.

As a professional diplomat, Dulles had some reason to have

looked back with some regret at this technical performance in the days immediately after Stalin's death, as Goold-Adams suggests he did.

There is an even larger issue—or question—embedded in this story. The secretary of state is an important official in the executive branch—next to the president and the vice-president, the most important official. But he is appointed by the president, does not submit himself to the electorate, and serves at the president's pleasure. Like everyone else in the executive branch except the president and vice-president, he is, in the best sense, a hired hand. His duty is to advise the president, understand as profoundly and sympathetically as he can the reasons for the president's decision, and then execute the letter and spirit of that decision, unless he chooses to resign.

The simple fact is that Dulles resisted the president's impulse to speak out promptly after Stalin's death, agreed only when he found unanticipated pressures in Europe for a Western peace gesture and negotiation with Moscow, and then delivered a speech, two days after the president's, which appeared to undercut the spirit if not the letter of what Eisenhower had said on April 16.

In the case of Byrnes' rejection of Acheson and Clayton's recommendation of April 1946 (*The Division of Europe after World War II: 1946*), there was no recourse to the president. In this case, Dulles undoubtedly spoke to Eisenhower a good many times between March 4 and April 10, when the former went on vacation. It is probable that Dulles' speech of April 18 was submitted and agreed to by Eisenhower, although the relevant speech file in Dulles' papers does not indicate that such clearance took place.[45] But Dulles was scrupulous— almost obsessive—in his efforts to keep in step with the president; and Eisenhower's operating style in the military and in politics had systematically involved acquiring a tough deputy who would deliver the unpleasant messages, leaving to Eisenhower both freedom of action and a more amiable posture; for example, Walter Bedell Smith, Lucius Clay, Alfred Gruenther, and Sherman Adams all performed this role. Eisenhower was quite capable of judging it operationally useful for his secretary of state to make a speech in the wake of his, reminding both Moscow and America's allies that there was a great deal of business in which momentum had to be maintained while we awaited the outcome of whatever peaceful responses the new Soviet leadership might be prepared to make to his speech.

On the other hand, there is some reason to believe that there was, in fact, an incomplete meeting of minds between Eisenhower and Dulles in the wake of Stalin's death. Eisenhower sensed immediately that men and women in the United States and everywhere else, skeptical as they might have been, still ached for peace and asked: "Is this a moment when things could be changed for the better?" However small the opportunities for any fundamental change in relations between Moscow and the West were reckoned to be by qualified experts, that popular feeling was a force with which professional diplomacy had to reckon. The secretary of state should have been capable of responding to his president's sensitivity to this powerful sentiment and of swiftly adjusting his approach to EDC and other matters to take it into account. But I suspect Dulles interpreted Eisenhower's correct political instinct in March 1953 as a weakness he was later to articulate to C. D. Jackson at a private dinner on July 11, 1955, shortly before he left for the Geneva summit conference:

> . . . what I am most worried about is the President. He and I have a relationship, both personal and operating, that has rarely existed between a Secretary of State and his President. As you know, I have nothing but admiration and respect for him, both as a person and as a man aware of foreign policy and conference pitfalls. Yet he is so inclined to be humanly generous, to accept a superficial tactical smile as evidence of inner warmth, that he might in a personal moment with the Russians accept a promise or a proposition at face value and

upset the apple cart. Don't forget that informal buffet dinners will be the regular procedure every day, at which time I estimate the real work will be done, and it is at that time that I am particularly afraid that the Russians may get in their "real work" with the President. . . .

The President likes things to be right, and pleasant, between people. He tires when an unpleasantness is dragged out indefinitely.[46]

Eisenhower's somewhat symmetrical assessment of Dulles is set down in an entry in his diary for May 14, 1953.

He is not particularly persuasive in presentation and, at times, seems to have a curious lack of understanding of how his words and manner may affect another personality. Personally, I like and admire him; my only doubts concerning him lie in the general field of personality, not in his capacity as a student of foreign affairs.[47]

Thus, elements of personality helped prevent the emergence of a fully coherent American policy in the wake of Stalin's death. Despite the almost compulsive detail of the communications between Eisenhower and Dulles, their minds did not quite meet. Their relationship evokes something of a Victorian novel in which two characters, closely aligned, cannot quite communicate the deepest thoughts in their minds.

There is no firm reason to believe that, if Dulles had designed a diplomatic track responsive to the president's instinct and taken the initiative on Germany and other matters promptly after Stalin's death, the outcome would have been greatly different. Certainly, the tactical position of the United States and the West would have been stronger, but a unified Germany and an end to the military confrontation in the center of Europe might have eluded negotiations in the spring of 1953 as they did early in 1954. We shall never know.

What the story illuminates is the power over the behavior of men in public life of the often unarticulated images they carry in their heads, including their images of each other; and, as in the earlier books in the series, this essay suggests the critical importance of timing: two months or so lost for the attack on German oil in 1944, a year or so lost in 1946–1947 before confronting Stalin on both Germany and the offer of large-scale American aid in reconstruction, nine months or so lost before representatives of the West met with the representative of Stalin's successors—and not at the summit. Of course, earlier is not always better. In these three cases I am still inclined to believe it would have been better. In the rhythms of public life there may emerge a moment for an idea when its time has come, and it is translated into action; but that moment may not necessarily be the moment of greatest opportunity. The unambiguous point is that, one way or the other, timing matters.

Appendix A

The March 6, 1953, Draft of the Proposed "Message" and Related Documents

[*Note*: This appendix includes the March 6 draft of the proposed presidential "Message" and the "supporting thinking," as presented to the March 11 NSC meeting; the major changes made in the March 11 draft "Message," with alternative tailpieces for delivery in a television studio to an American audience or before the U.N. General Assembly; and a draft cable to Churchill and other Western European leaders for delivery two days before release of the "Message." Appendix A concludes with Eisenhower's cable to Churchill, dispatched at 7:39 P.M., March 11, incorporating his three basic decisions of the day: rejecting the summit meeting proposed by Churchill; indicating his inclination to make a speech soon, "giving to the world some promise of hope"; and keeping open the option of a summit meeting including the U.K., the U.S., and "probably the French." (The verbatim text of the cable to Churchill is from the Dwight D. Eisenhower Papers, Ann Whitman File, International Series, box 16, "President–Churchill, Jan.–May 1953" folder 5, Dwight D. Eisenhower Library. The rest of the material is from the C. D. Jackson Papers, box 85, "Stalin's Death Speech" folder, Dwight D. Eisenhower Library.)]

Draft 1, Presented to
NSC March 11
Written night of March 6
A Message to the Soviet Government and the Russian Peoples
The death of Joseph V. Stalin ends an era in your history and in the history of the world. I send this message in the faith and hope

that, acting together with other nations, we can now move forward towards peace.

In the years since 1929, the Russian peoples, under Stalin's leadership, achieved great economic advance. They defended themselves with courage and success against a foreign aggressor. The Russian peoples of this generation have kept alive the Russian cultural heritage which belongs to us all. The world respects those achievements.

But our tie is stronger than respect. We shared as allies the struggle of the Second World War. I was a soldier in that war. I knew your soldiers as comrades in arms. I am convinced that in 1945 the Russian peoples shared with those of the United States and the rest of the world these aspirations: peace, economic progress, the right to live our lives freely and without fear, with our families, each in the manner of his own community. These aspirations have not been fulfilled; but they remain the common aspirations of all mankind.

At the end of the Second World War Russian and American troops met in the center of Europe. We were there because our nations had been attacked and we defended ourselves. We each had the right to be there. More than that, we had the right to insure that it would not happen again. Concretely, our people and yours share with some three hundred million citizens of Europe this common objective: that the Continent of Europe never again be dominated by a single power.

There were two ways to seek our future security in Europe after 1945. We could agree effectively to control the armaments of Europe and our own armaments in such a way as to remove the danger of aggression. If we did this, then the life of the whole great continent of Europe could rise again and its peoples would be at liberty to develop their economy, their political life, and their culture as they wished. This was the American aim. It remains the American aim.

The other way to seek security was to hold and control the territories occupied by our armies. This was the way chosen by the Soviet Government. It has required that the Soviet Government dominate in detail the lives of other countries, against the will of their peoples. It has endangered the rest of the world. It has not brought security to the Russian peoples.

In the face of this Soviet policy of unilateral domination, we have sought to build a coalition. It is a coalition of responsible equals, working together to defend themselves, to develop their economies and their political life, in ways arising from their respective cultures. We have conducted our affairs in full consistency with the letter and spirit of the United Nations' charter. With this coalition of the Free World, we have shared, and share today, a basic aspiration: that we may be joined as soon as possible by those outside, so that the full purposes of the United Nations—which we helped create together—may be fulfilled.

It is a clear lesson of this century that no nation can achieve security by itself. This we have learned from two World Wars in which the losses of Russia were greater than for any other nation. This, above all, is the meaning of the new weapons that mankind has in its hands. There is no other way than to seek our security together.

This cannot be done by words. It can only be achieved by effective measures, agreed in common, and enforced by means that we all can trust.

I propose, therefore, that the foreign ministers of Great Britain, France, the Soviet Union, and the United States (consider UN alternative) meet in the near future, at a time mutually to be agreed. I intend that the United States shall lay before that meeting concrete proposals. These proposals will be wholly consistent with the legitimate security interests of our respective countries. They will aim to free the continent of Europe to develop a peaceful, unified life.

The United States shall also lay before this meeting proposals for joint action designed to end the war in Korea. So long as the Korean war continues, there is no sound basis for movement towards larger common goals.

The United States shall propose measures for the general control of armaments and special security arrangements for Europe.

The United States shall propose measures for the unification of Germany by free elections as well as proposals designed to end the occupation of Austria. We believe that, within a structure of general and regional security and economic arrangements, a Germany unified by democratic means would constitute a creative force in Europe, without danger to East or West.

Our armament programs draw from the world economy resources needed not only for ourselves but which are required to develop the economies of many nations whose economic resources are underdeveloped. They seek economic progress not only for its own sake, but also to make good in human dignity their political independence, in many cases hard-earned and freshly won. In facing the grave problems of our own security, we must bear in mind the cost to these nations of the present world tension and we must bear in mind our responsibilities to them. As we succeed in reducing the burden of armaments which now bears upon us, the United States stands ready to consider measures to enlarge its contribution to the development of underdeveloped areas.

You should understand that two firm intentions underlie this American initiative. First, we shall agree to no action with respect to any nation without the participation of representatives of that nation in our negotiations. Second, the United States will in no way relax its efforts to develop its own strength and that of its allies, until alternative effective measures of collective security have been agreed and put into effect.

It would be foolhardy to disguise from each other or from the peoples of the world the difficulty of the common task I propose. We must remake eight years of bad history. We must find the means to ensure the security of our respective nations without dominating the lives of other peoples. I undertake this initiative because I believe profoundly that the true interests and objectives of our nations are wholly compatible with this result.

Presented NSC

March 11

Supporting Thinking for Message to Soviet Government and Russian Peoples

This first draft of a message to the Soviet Government and the Russian peoples is based on the following general considerations:

1. Stalin's death has produced within the Soviet Union and throughout the Communist bloc great emotional shock. This extends to friend and foe, to self-serving bureaucrat and enthusiast, to peasant and worker. In a fashion unique to modern times, Stalin, as a symbol of authority, temporal and spiritual, has been built into the

life of the citizens of Communist areas despite themselves. Neither Malenkov nor any other figure now alive can fill this gap in the immediate future. The shock effect will undoubtedly diminish with time. Over the next days, however, it constitutes a unique Soviet vulnerability.

2. In its response to the present situation, the Soviet regime is likely to make an effort to bridge the emotional and ideological gap which Stalin's death will create throughout the Communist bloc. The regime will see it as vital to prevent the emergence of the notion that Stalin's death opens up fresh options in Soviet internal and external policy. As in the case of Lenin's death the regime is likely to invoke Stalin's name in justification for all its major acts. It is a major American interest to make the peoples of the Communist world see Stalin's death as the end of an era and not as part of a continuing line of development.

3. It is a hypothesis not without basis in intelligence that there has been a split within the top levels of Soviet power on the appropriate Soviet policy towards the external world. Malenkov, along with Stalin, is believed to have held the view that nothing very much need be done, except to persist in present Soviet policies; and that schisms in the camp of the Free World would present themselves for Soviet exploitation. Others are believed to have held the view that, beneath the surface of its vacillations and setbacks, the Free World was moving toward a unity which had to be met with either force or diplomatic accommodation. If this intelligence conclusion is correct, the initiative proposed would maximize the chances that this policy division would rise again within the Soviet regime and contribute to difficulties in the stable disposition of Stalin's power.

4. There is also some intelligence basis for believing that elements high in the Soviet bureaucracy would be prepared to see an accommodation to the external world, if it did not violate Russian national interests in the limited sense. The proposed initiative would maximize the chances that these men might act to make their views effective; and it might contribute, in the case of elements in the Soviet armed forces, to a willingness to participate in a struggle for Stalin's power, should Malenkov have not yet succeeded in its consolidation.

5. Such an alternative would help solidify the Free World in its future relations to the Communist bloc.

6. The acute but temporary traumatic state of emotion in the Soviet Union and the Communist bloc gives to the US the possibility of seizing a general initiative in the cold war. If we are prepared to mobilize all arms of American policy in line with this initiative, and to sustain a consistent set of actions, there is no reason why the initiative cannot be held.

7. *If these purposes are to be fulfilled, it is essential that the initiative have serious diplomatic substance, and be developed with full professional diplomatic skill, even if the chances of immediate success in negotiation are rated nil.* Nothing would destroy its effect more thoroughly than the conviction inside the Kremlin and in the Free World that we were *merely* playing psychological tricks. The proposals must be serious and must be consistent with American interests and objectives. We must be prepared to back our play.

The text of the draft incorporates the following specific judgments and considerations:

1. Although Soviet postwar policy must be dealt with, this would not appear to be a useful occasion to express fully our views concerning the late leader. Thus the restrained tone of the references to Stalin.

2. It is fundamental to this initiative that we are trying to strike the Russian peoples and the peoples of the Communist bloc, at a moment of emotional indecision and even bewilderment, with a new vision of possibilities. It appears important, therefore, to emphasize those strands which unite rather than divide them from the rest of the world. Thus the references of respect to Soviet economic and military achievement, as well as to the Russian (not Soviet) cultural heritage. Thus, also, the emphasis on our war-time alliance.

3. Given the possibility that some close to power in the Soviet Union think more in terms of the Russian national interest than in terms of ideology and the expansion of Soviet power, it appears important to recognize the elements of legitimacy in the Russian security interest. Thus, the presentation of the Russian security interest in Europe.

4. The forum for the proposed diplomatic conference could be: a meeting of the heads of state of the Big Four; a meeting of the foreign ministers of the Big Four; a meeting of the Security Council of the UN; or some larger UN grouping. This is a matter, of course, for only the highest diplomatic judgment. My instinct is for some version of the Big Four, in the first instance.

5. The listing of proposals for the meeting is meant to strike a balance between the need for concreteness in this initiative on the one hand and the danger of over-elaborate commitment on the other.

6. The suggestion about the contribution to the underdeveloped areas should be noted. Nothing could help more in solidifying those areas within the Free World than a belief

a) that the United States sincerely sought peace; and

b) that the scale of our contribution to their economic development hinged on success in effectively reducing and controlling armaments.

Properly developed and exploited in subsequent US information policy, this proposal might develop an attractiveness equivalent to the Marshall Plan initiated in June 1947.

7. The problem of China has been explicitly left out of this approach because of the evident complexity of the position created by the Korean war. With respect to the Korean war and the proposed conference, what I have in mind here is our pressing upon the Soviet Union some version of the Indians' UN resolution and pressing upon them, as well, a cessation of armament deliveries to Korea.

8. It is envisaged that a message of this kind should be delivered after Stalin's funeral, perhaps the day after the funeral. Given the Russian concern for formality, and our interest in underlining the seriousness of the initiative, it would be advantageous to let them have this message a day before its open publication. The same applies with equal or greater force to our major allies. If it is envisaged that a special Presidential representative shall be sent to Stalin's funeral, he might also deliver this message in the President's name.

9. This message should also be delivered, straight-face, in high seriousness to the satellite governments.

Draft 2
March 11
Major Changes in the Message post-NSC meeting of March 11

I intend, therefore, that the representatives of the United States press on vigorously with concrete measures looking towards peace.

What is it that the United States is seeking?

The United States seeks measures for the effective control of armaments including weapons of mass destruction.

The United States seeks measures for the unification of Germany by free elections as well as proposals designed to end the occupation of Austria. We believe that, within a structure of appropriate security and economic arrangements, a Germany unified by democratic means within a unified Europe would constitute a creative force, without danger to East or West.

Our armament programs draw from the world economy resources needed by our peoples. In your country the economic progress achieved in recent decades has not yet benefited substantially the welfare of the Russian peoples.

More than that, the Soviet government prevented in 1947 the joining of the peoples of Russia and Eastern Europe in common European measures for reconstruction, and denied them the benefits of American economic assistance. The Soviet government has systematically prevented the development of peaceful trade between the areas it controlled and the outside world. . . .

It is self-evident, however, that we cannot move seriously, either as Americans alone or in concert with other nations, including your nation, toward these larger objectives—the underlying goals of all mankind—until the wars which are going on in Asia are definitely ended. I look to the Government of the Soviet Union for the indispensable evidence of its sincerity, namely, action to end the wars in Korea and Indo-China. An armistice in Korea or in Indo-China whose sole beneficial result would be to produce a cease-fire, with real peace not even dimly discernible, does not constitute the "indispensable evidence" I refer to. The Government of the Soviet Union can give that evidence if it so wishes.

Lest there be any misunderstanding, I tell you now that with respect to the prisoner of war issue, the Government of the United States continues to be willing to stand by the proposal of the Government of India, which was agreed to within the United Nations by a vast majority of the world's Governments.

And lest there be further misunderstanding, I say to you with all the emphasis at my command, that until these wars are ended, and until we have together gone on to create effective measures of collective security which we can trust, the United States will in no way relax its efforts to develop its own strength and that of its allies. . . .

(Tail piece if delivered in studio)

* * *

I should now like to say a few words to the American people.

This initiative is not a short term, diplomatic maneuver, designed to exploit Stalin's death. It springs from my own convictions, long held, laid before you on many occasions. I intend that my Administration shall actively seek peace, with all arms of policy working together, not for days or months but for years if necessary. I have launched this initiative because my own conviction coincides, I believe, with the desires not only of the American people, but also with the desires of the peoples of the free world and with the desires of those now living under totalitarian domination.

We may not achieve results quickly, although fresh action is already under way. But I do intend that we get results.

There is one thought I would leave with you tonight above any other. It is a condition for the success of our new enterprise that the American people exhibit a high degree of unity and that they give unremitting support to our security measures at home and abroad.

The Free World must exhibit new capacities for unity and common action. It would be fatal to our purposes if the launching of this initiative were taken as an occasion for slackened effort or for a weakening in the bonds which unite the Free World. Strong words spoken without strength of unity convey little beyond self-deception.

When we meet the Soviet Government around the conference tables of the United Nations and elsewhere, we shall continue to negotiate in good faith. We are prepared to consider all serious proposals for peace in Korea and Indo-China and for releasing the life of Europe from the unbearable tension it has borne since 1945.

But in the meanwhile, until the very day when alternative arrangements for peace and collective security are ready to be put into operation, we must press on with the building of military, political, and economic strength at home and thoughout the Free World.

(Tail piece for U.N. Delivery)

[*Note*: As above, except for the following final paragraph.]

In the end, when we are successful, the United Nations will come fully into its own, fulfilling the high purposes written imperishably into its Charter. In the meanwhile, it is an indispensable instrument for us all. It continues to have my full support.

> DRAFT—Eisenhower–Churchill, to be dispatched two days before delivery of message, one day before delivery of text to governments.

My dear Churchill (or Winston or Mr. Prime Minister):

I have decided to deliver a message to the Soviet Government and the Russian peoples on March ——. This message will propose that the Council of Foreign Ministers meet at an early convenient date; and that the United States, with its allies, lay on the table concrete proposals for the settlement of outstanding issues in Korea, Germany, Austria, as well as positions on the control of armaments. I shall transmit the text of the message to you tomorrow, March ——.

I have been acutely aware of the implications of this initiative for the Western alliance. I wish to assure you forthwith that, of course, I expect that you, the French, and ourselves would work together in greatest intimacy in the preparations for such a conference if, indeed, the Soviet government accepts the offer.

I wish, further, to emphasize a view I know you share; that a minimum condition for the success of this initiative is the maintenance of momentum—if possible accelerated momentum—in the affairs of the alliance, notably with respect to EDC. We would be foolish to count on a major diplomatic result soon; although we must seek such a result with the greatest seriousness. We have a duty, however, to present our peaceful proposals to the Soviet government and the Russian peoples at this juncture in history; to dramatize the willingness of the Free World to seek the peace; and to clarify out of the negotiations, should they fail, the precise nature and meaning of the Soviet obstruction, and thus further to unite the Free World.

The decision to proceed without prior consultation with you and the French in proposing the meeting has been painful. I am, as you well know, deeply committed to the Western alliance. I have weighed the disadvantages of moving alone in the first instance against the advantages of promptness and sharpness of impact. There may, too, be advantages for us all in having this initiative arise unilaterally from the United States, given the interpretation many people in the Free World have placed on the apparent unwillingness of the United States boldly to face Soviet representatives across the conference table in recent years.

In the end I was moved by a conviction that, on balance, this was an initiative the people of my own country and the peoples and governments of the Free World would wish me to take. (You, more than most, know the loneliness of the decisions the President must sometimes take.)

I wish finally to make clear that I do not regard this initiative as a short-term psychological trick. I have long held the view that peace must be pursued positively and by sustained acts, taken with the allies of the United States. I believe it within the wit of our diplomacy simultaneously to bind up and maintain the unity of the Free World while holding forth to the governments and peoples of the Communist bloc a concrete vision of the peaceful alternative we seek.

I would welcome an exchange of views with you on our next steps in common.

SANITIZED COPY
Department of State
1953 MAR 11 PM 7 39
VERBATIM TEXT
SENT TO: Amembassy LONDON PRIORITY 6047
EYES ONLY HOLMES.
Pls deliver immediately fol msg from President to Churchill:
QTE The subject raised in your message of today has been engaging our attention here for some days. We are convinced that a move

giving to the world some promise of hope, which will have the virtues of simplicity and persuasiveness, should be made quickly. A number of ideas have been advanced, but none of them has been completely acceptable.

QTE At our meeting in New York I by no means meant to reject the possibility that the leaders of the West might sometime have to make some collective move if we are to achieve progress in lessening the world's tensions.

QTE However, even now I tend to doubt the wisdom of a formal multilateral meeting since this would give our opponent the same kind of opportunity he has so often had to use such a meeting simultaneously to balk every reasonable effort of ourselves and to make of the whole occurrence another propaganda mill for the Soviet. It is entirely possible, however, that your government and ourselves, and probably the French, should agree upon some general purpose and program under which each would have a specific part to play.

QTE I am sure that Foster Dulles will attempt to keep in rather close touch with Anthony regarding possibilities and any tentative conclusions we may reach.

QTE Warm regards.

QTE Signed Ike UNQTE

Appendix B

The Provisional CIA Estimate of the Consequences of Stalin's Death

[*Note*: The provisional CIA estimate of the probable consequences of Stalin's death contains the prescient conclusion that the Western European leaders would hope for "at least a temporary relaxation of tensions and enable them to postpone disagreeable policy decisions." (From the C. D. Jackson Records, box 5, "Stalin's Death—PSB Plans for Exploitation of" folder, Dwight D. Eisenhower Library.)]

CENTRAL INTELLIGENCE AGENCY

10 March 1953

SE-39: PROBABLE CONSEQUENCES OF THE DEATH OF STALIN AND OF THE ELEVATION OF MALENKOV TO LEADERSHIP IN THE USSR

I. *THE INITIAL TRANSFER OF AUTHORITY*

1. The problem of transfer of power is one of the most difficult which the Soviet system could face. The important initial step, the formal transfer of authority, with Malenkov as titular leader, has apparently been effected with remarkable rapidity and precision. The smoothness of the transfer of authority and the speed with which the Government and Party posts were filled, suggest an acute awareness on the part of the Soviet leaders of the dangers inherent

in the situation,* and that necessary plans to bring about the change were prepared, at least in outline, well in advance of Stalin's death.

2. Malenkov's key position in the Soviet Communist Party throughout the past fourteen years, his conspicuous and apparently planned elevation since 1948, his prominent role at and since the 19th Party Congress, and the accolade accorded him by Beria at Stalin's funeral suggest that there will be no immediate challenge to his position. However, we cannot estimate whether he has the qualities of leadership necessary to consolidate his position and to attain unchallenged power, since he has always operated with the backing of Stalin. Neither is it possible to estimate with confidence the capabilities or probable courses of action of his possible opponents.

3. A struggle for power could develop within the Soviet hierarchy at any time. Given the nature of the Soviet state, such a struggle would probably be carried on within the Party organization and higher echelons of the bureaucracy. In any case, the peoples of the USSR are unlikely to participate actively in the struggle. Even if a struggle should break out in the near future, we believe that the hold of the Communist Party over the USSR is not likely to be shaken quickly. We do not believe that such a struggle would in itself lead the rulers of the USSR deliberately to initiate general war.*

*In the new organization, Malenkov apparently now holds the same titular position within the Presidium and the Secretariat of the Party and in the Council of Ministers which Stalin held. In the Council of Ministers, power has been concentrated in the hands of Malenkov as Chairman and four First Deputy Chairmen: Beria, Molotov, Bulganin, and Kaganovich. These five make up the Presidium of the Council of Ministers. It may be significant that this body closely parallels in nature and membership the wartime Committee of State Defense under Stalin. The concentration of power has been increased, and the top party and government organs have been reduced in number and size. The new organization of Party and Government and the extensive reorganization and merger of several major industries under Malenkov appear to tighten and streamline the administrative system.

*The Deputy Director for Intelligence, The Joint Staff, believes that paragraph 3 should read as follows: "A struggle for power could develop within the Soviet hierarchy at any time. Given the nature of the Soviet state, such a struggle would probably be carried on within the Party

II. *PROBABLE CONSEQUENCES OF DEATH OF STALIN*

A. *Effects on the Bases of Soviet Power*

4. The economic and military bases of Soviet power are unlikely to be immediately affected by Stalin's death. However, the new leadership may prove less successful in maintaining and strenthening these bases of Soviet power.

5. The effect of Western diplomatic or psychological moves on Soviet stability and strength cannot be estimated without knowledge of the contemplated moves. However, we believe that the USSR is politically more vulnerable today than before Stalin's death. The new leadership will have difficult policy decisions to face, and these difficulties may be increased by personal rivalries for power which would reduce Soviet strength and the cohesion of the international Communist movement.

B. *Future Soviet Policies*

6. In the near future, the new Soviet leadership will almost certainly pursue the foreign and domestic policies established during recent years. In particular, it will probably continue to emphasize unremitting hostility to the West (including the tactic of splitting the West), the enlargement of the Bloc economic base, and the increase of Bloc military power.

7. The death of Stalin removes an autocrat who, while ruthless and determined to spread Soviet power, did not allow his ambitions to lead him into reckless courses of action in his foreign policy. It would be unsafe to assume that the new Soviet regime will have Stalin's skill in avoiding general war. At least initially, the regime will also lack his freedom of action and his ability to maneuver, since it will not possess Stalin's immense prestige and authority. Specifically, in foreign policy, the new regime will probably find it more difficult to abandon positions than did Stalin and might feel itself compelled to react more strongly if moves of the West confronted it with the need for major decisions. Conversely, the new leadership will prob-

---

organization. However, any serious disagreement could well have much more widespread effects, involving the Army or large sections of the population. If such a struggle should break out in the near future, we believe that the hold of the Communist Party over the USSR is not likely to be shaken quickly. So long as the struggle is confined within the Kremlin, we do not believe that it would lead the rulers of the USSR deliberately to initiate general war."

ably exercise caution in the near future in taking action which it thought would force the West to make comparable decisions. If the West should suggest re-examination of the principal issues which have divided East and West, the new Soviet government would probably adhere to established Soviet positions. However, the new government would probably show a less sure hand in dealing with new issues or in handling new Western proposals.*

8. The new Soviet regime probably fears that, while it is in the process of consolidating its power, the West may make aggressive moves against the Bloc. It would probably view with extreme suspicion any new moves made by the West, particularly those involving long-range air forces or military forces close to the Bloc frontiers.

C. *Effects upon the Peoples of the USSR*

9. The death of Stalin removes the man who had been built up to the status of a demi-god. To many of the people of the USSR, he was the man of steel who had raised Russia to industrial and military power, who had withstood the German attack, and who had led the peoples of the USSR to the greatest military victory in Russian history. Stalin's death will be a psychological shock to large numbers of Soviet people. However, we estimate that this shock in itself will not affect the stability of the new regime.

D. *Effect upon the Bloc and the International Communist Movement*

10. For some time, no successor to Stalin will be able to achieve comparable status or similar significance as a symbol of the international Communist movement and as the undisputed leader

---

*The Deputy Director for Intelligence, The Joint Staff, believes that paragraph 7 should read: "The death of Stalin removes an autocrat who, while ruthless and determined to spread Soviet power, chose courses of action which although causing the Western world to rearm, did not result in general war during his lifetime. It would be unsafe to assume that the new Soviet leadership will either desire or be able to choose courses of action that will avoid precipitation of all-out war. At least initially, the Soviet regime may lack freedom of action and the ability to maneuver since he does not possess Stalin's immense prestige and authority. On the other hand, particularly in relation to foreign policy, the new regime may find it more difficult to abandon positions than did Stalin and might feel itself compelled to react more strongly to moves of the West. If the West should suggest re-examination of the principal issues which have divided East and West, the new Soviet government would probably outwardly adhere to established Soviet positions."

of world Communism. This may have some effect on the rank and file, at least temporarily, but the cohesion of the hard core of the Communist movement outside the Bloc is not likely to be impaired. If there should be a struggle for power within the Soviet Communist Party, the cohesion of the Communist movement outside the Bloc would almost certainly be weakened.

11. Kremlin control over the European Satellites is so firm that we do not believe it will be impaired merely by the death of Stalin. However, in the unlikely event that a struggle in the Soviet Communist Party should spread to the Soviet Army and the Soviet Security Forces, Soviet control over the Satellites would almost certainly be shaken.

12. Relations between Tito and Moscow are unlikely to change as a result of the death of Stalin. The antagonism was not personal, but arose from a genuine clash of Yugoslav national interests with the Soviet Communist Party. Moreover, both sides have taken actions and adopted positions which would be extremely difficult to reverse. The Kremlin could not recognize Tito as an independent Communist ally without undermining its position with the European Satellites.

13. We do not believe that Tito's influence within the Satellites or within Communist Parties outside the Bloc will increase, unless there should be a prolonged struggle for power in the USSR.

14. We believe that Stalin's death will have no immediate effect upon Sino-Soviet cooperation or upon Chinese Communist foreign policies. However, no successor to Stalin will have prestige and authority in Asia comparable to his. The future of Mao as leader and theoretician of Asian Communism will inevitably increase with the disappearance of the former supreme leader. Mao will almost certainly have more influence in the determination of Bloc policy affecting Asia. He almost certainly will not seek leadership of the international Communist movement. The new Moscow leadership will probably deal cautiously with Mao; if it does not, serious strains in Sino-Soviet relations will almost certainly develop.

III. *PROBABLE WESTERN REACTION TO DEATH OF STALIN AND ELEVATION OF MALENKOV*

15. We believe that in general the Western European leaders will be disposed for the time being to conduct the East-West strug-

gle with greater hesitancy and caution. They will probably fear that any immediate Western pressure on the Bloc would increase the danger of war and facilitate the stabilization of authority in the USSR. They will also probably hope that, if Western pressure is not exerted, the problems involved in the consolidation of the authority of the new regime of the USSR will bring about at least a temporary relaxation of tensions and enable them to postpone disagreeable policy decisions.

Appendix C

Extracts from the Author's Notes on the Origin of the President's Speech of April 16, 1953

[*Note*: These extracts from notes on the origin of the president's speech of April 16, 1953, were set down by the author at C. D. Jackson's request and sent to him on May 11, 1953.]

The purpose of these notes is to supply that limited portion of the record of events known to me leading up to the delivery of the President's speech of April 16, 1953. It should be borne in mind throughout that my knowledge is partial. The record can only be filled out by others, particularly by Mr. C. D. Jackson. . . .

In the week before Stalin died, Rostow had arranged that Millikan and he call on Jackson on the afternoon of March 11, to discuss the future relations between CENIS and the various agencies of the government; and we were, at this time, arranging that CENIS make its contribution to the W. Jackson Committee. [The committee, set up with William Jackson as chairman, was to advise Eisenhower on the appropriate organization of psychological warfare.]

The Week of March 4–12

Early on Wednesday morning, March 4, Millikan received a telephone call from Robert Amory of the CIA asking that CENIS prepare an intelligence appreciation of the situation created by Stalin's grave illness, which had just been announced. In particular, four questions were to be answered:

1. Is Stalin dead?
2. What are the likely dispositions of Soviet power?
3. What are the likely changes in external policy, if any?
4. What are the likely relations of the new regime to Mao?

Millikan, Richard Hatch, Francis Bator, James Cross and Rostow, at CENIS, discussed these questions from 10 A.M. to shortly before noon. A draft was prepared by Rostow and revised by all. It was dispatched to Washington by courier Wednesday night.

It was unanimously decided in CENIS that we would not only submit an intelligence appreciation but also a statement of the key vulnerability created by Stalin's death and suggestions for prompt American action to exploit that vulnerability. In general the suggestion consisted in the opening of a political warfare offensive of the kind envisaged in the Vulnerability report, spearheaded by an American initiated meeting of the major powers, to be offered by the President. It was also decided that, in view of the work we had done at taxpayers' expense for a year and a half on this problem, we had a duty to call our suggestion to the attention of C. D. Jackson. The operational suggestion was abstracted from the general intelligence appreciation and was sent to Jackson, also on Wednesday night. We informed Amory by telephone of our having done this on our own initiative.

On Thursday, March 5, at about 3 P.M. Jackson called Rostow. He indicated that he had received both the communication to him and the full appreciation sent to the CIA. He indicated that he, too, felt that now was the time to open a general political warfare offensive; and he requested that Rostow come to Washington, arriving, if possible, at about 3 o'clock on the afternoon of March 6.

Rostow arrived at Jackson's office about 3:15 on March 6. He was informed:

(a) that Charles Wilson of General Electric had recently suggested to the President that he initiate a peace move, or meeting. J. F. Dulles' reaction to this suggestion was not unfavorable. Although coming during the period of Stalin's illness, Dulles noted that conditions had changed;

(b) that the NSC had issued a directive instructing the CIA to prepare an intelligence appreciation of the position created by Stalin's death by Monday, March 9; that the State Department indicate its appreciation and suggestions for action; and C. D. Jackson produce a plan to exploit Stalin's death also by Monday, March 9.

Jackson indicated that he had a small staff, headed by George Morgan of the PSB [Psychological Strategy Board], helping him on the general follow-up exploitation of Stalin's death. The Staff was drawn as a group of individuals from various parts of the government and was already at work on Friday, March 6. It was generally understood that outside help would be used by Jackson and Rostow's presence in Washington was known to this group.

Jackson asked Rostow what he had to add to the message sent from Cambridge. Rostow replied that he had a reasonably clear idea as to what the President ought to say and had some suggestions as to how an initial move might be exploited. Jackson instructed Rostow to produce three drafts: a Presidential statement; a rationale for that statement; and any suggestions that he might have for a follow-up plan.

Jackson then departed for a scheduled discussion of these matters, which included Nitze and Bohlen of the Department of State and Emmet Hughes of the White House staff.

Rostow was installed by 3:45 P.M. on March 6 in room 242½ at the Old State Department Building and equipped with an excellent secretary, Mrs. Bridges. At about 11:30 P.M., drafts were finished for all three items requested by Mr. Jackson. Mrs. Bridges typed for several further hours the dictated portion of the suggestions for the follow-up plan and arranged that these be available to Jackson from 8 A.M. on the morning of Saturday, March 7.

On Saturday, March 7th, Jackson arrived and went through these three documents. He called in Emmet Hughes to read them. They found themselves in general accord with the Presidential statement and the case for it.

It was then decided by Hughes and Jackson that, with one exception, the Presidential draft would be shown to no one until Monday. The reasons for this were the absence from town of certain key figures, notably John Foster Dulles, and the danger that might arise if the draft were put through the conventional bureaucratic machinery for clearance: dangers both of security and dilution. Rostow hazarded the view that if the President were to act in this matter promptly, he would have to take the decision on his own, in a rather lonely manner.

The three sets of papers were, however, shown to George Morgan on the afternoon of Saturday, March 7, by Mr. Jackson. Morgan was told that he should assume, in the paper he and the staff were preparing, that the opening gun in the political warfare campaign would be a Presidential statement of some sort; and this was all that he was to tell his own working staff and to include in their paper. On a personal basis, however, he was shown the Presidential draft. Rostow had lunch with Morgan and gave him the third paper; that is, notes for the follow-up plan. Rostow indicated that these were meant to be simply notes for the use of Morgan's staff and that he had no desire to peddle them elsewhere. Morgan noted, however, that Rostow had felt free to include diplomacy fully in the follow-up plan, whereas his terms of reference largely excluded diplomatic policy. For that reason he urged that the draft be "shown to others" by Rostow.

On Monday, March 9, it became evident that there would be opposition to the Presidential statement from the Department of State. Jackson had described the meeting on March 6 to Rostow as having gone round and round in circles, but having emerged with agreement on this point: that only a proposal for a four-power conference would give adequate substance to a Presidential act at this time. And it had then appeared not impossible that Nitze and Bohlen would go along with Hughes and Jackson. Nevertheless, Bohlen and Nitze raised important objections on Monday afternoon, when the draft of the Presidential statement and the rationale for it were shown to them by Hughes.

The major business for Jackson on March 9 was to cope with a long paper prepared by Morgan and his special team. This outlined a great many psychological warfare actions as follow-up for the Presidential statement. This paper was circulated on Monday to all the relevant agencies in the government represented on the PSB. In view of the length of the document and the fact that it was under review in the government, it was agreed that an extremely brief NSC directive should be drafted in the following sense: urging that a Presidential statement be given; creating a special *ad hoc* committee to oversee the execution of the follow-up plan; and attaching the Morgan draft plus the comments made upon it, for the *ad hoc* committee to consider as part of its working materials. Rostow drafted such a directive.

On Monday, March 9, it was also decided that the issue would come to a decision on Wednesday, March 11, at an NSC meeting, Dulles being out of town until the late afternoon of March 10.

On Tuesday, March 10, a letter from Bohlen arrived stating formally the objections of the Department of State up to the level of Under Secretary. This letter explicitly excluded Dulles, who was still in New York.

At Jackson's request, after extensive discussion, Rostow prepared for verbal presentation at the NSC by Jackson a brief on each of the objections raised.

In order to meet the State Department's view that the President's proposal would be a dangerous shock to our allies, it was proposed that Jackson prepare letters from the President to Churchill and Mayer to be sent two days before the speech, one day before the text was made available. Rostow prepared such drafts.

On Monday, March 9 (but perhaps also on Friday, March 6), Rostow had suggested to Jackson that he talk forthwith to George Kennan. Rostow heard Kennan's views on the night of Thursday, March 5, at the home of Millikan in Cambridge, and was impressed with the fact that they converged with those developed at CENIS and were sharply different from the views popularly attributed to Kennan as the author, if not the architect, of containment. Jackson immediately asked Kennan to come from his farm in Pennsylvania to Washington. Kennan saw Jackson for about an hour and a half between 2:30 and 4 o'clock on the afternoon of Tuesday, March 10. Rostow was present only for the period from about 3:15 to 4 o'clock. Kennan agreed that the kind of initiative suggested was the right course for the United States at this moment in history. He approved the draft statement in general, suggesting that it might be usefully nit-picked for detail by some of the old hands in the State Department. He indicated his view, now several years old, that the United States must positively support efforts to unify Germany and the continent; to create effective security measures there; and to engineer Russian and American military withdrawal, leaving behind a militarily safe, predominantly democratic and unified area. Kennan warned Jackson that taking this initiative required great clarity concerning its implications for Germany on the part of two men: the President and the Secretary of State. If this condition were fulfilled, there was no need to worry excessively about other opinions in Washington or about the short period of excitement in the foreign offices of Great Britain, France, and Bonn. Kennan expressed his faith that Washington would respond with great vigor and unity to the initiative, as it had to the Marshall Plan proposal; and that our allies would come along without much difficulty. Both Jackson and Rostow were moved by the combination of dignity, force, and eloquence with which Kennan presented his views, at a time when he obviously felt acutely his enforced divorce from events, as well as a profound desire to be useful to the country in these days when an understanding of Russia was as important as it had ever been before in our history. At one point Kennan explained that the initiative proposed by Jackson was designed to reverse the direction in which the wheel of diplomacy had been spinning for some years in Washington, and, taking him by the arms, said, 'you have the weight of the world on your shoulders. Good luck.' It should be noted that Jackson raised with Dulles the following day, March 11, the future of Kennan, and was told that it was his (Dulles') understanding that Kennan had tendered his resignation and that the matter was in the hands of Bedell Smith. Dulles' assistant later reported that the Secretary was loath to bring Kennan into the Department for fear of Congressional reaction.

Late on the night of March 10, Rostow was called to the office of Jackson to read over a letter Jackson had drafted to Dulles. The Secretary of State had arrived in town at about 4 o'clock on March 10 and had been met, according to rumor, by an excited group of his colleagues. Dulles had already asked to see Jackson at breakfast at 7:45 on Wednesday, March 11.

On Wednesday, March 11, Rostow saw Jackson at about 8:30 A.M., after his breakfast with Dulles. Jackson reported that Dulles had found the idea "intriguing," but had several reservations which he would have to think over before the 10:30 meeting of the National Security Council.

Rostow saw Jackson again as he emerged from the NSC meeting at about 12:30 P.M. Jackson announced that he did not know whether he was a man 'carrying a shield or being carried upon it.' He reported that

(a) he had had his full day in court;

(b) the President, remembering his experience with previous four-power meetings, was not enthusiastic about the Council of Foreign Ministers;

(c) Dulles took the position that our relations with France and Britain would be damaged by a unilateral initiative of this kind; that the governments of de Gasperi, Adenauer and Mayer would fall in a week; and that EDC would be postponed, if not destroyed. It was, nevertheless, agreed that a Presidential statement should be made and made soon, and that the bulk of the text as drafted was suitable.

Further, Stassen wished to see introduced into the speech a reference to the Marshall Plan and a recognition of the possibilities of drawing the East back toward the West, by economic means.

It may be recorded for history that the Secretary of Defense said at one point: 'I agree with Mr. Jackson; don't give the bastards anything but hope.'

It was further decided that the references to Korea would be expanded and a truce in Korea would be made even more clearly a condition for further movement towards the larger objectives of peace than the original draft had provided. Jackson was instructed to prepare a new text in the sense of the meeting.

While Jackson was at lunch on Wednesday, March 11, Rostow redrafted the message as instructed by Jackson. The essential device was to hold up a vision of the specific long-range objectives of American diplomacy but to make the negotiations designed to achieve that vision contingent upon a prior Korean settlement. [See Appendix A.]

Two tail pieces were added to the new draft, since it was envisaged that the President might deliver this statement either on television, to the American people, or to the U.N. Assembly on Thursday, March 19. These were drafted by Rostow, revised by Jackson. [See Appendix A.]

On Thursday, March 12, Jackson went to a luncheon meeting of the PSB. He found a warm welcome, appreciation for his effort of the previous day, and unanimity concerning the new draft. Bedell Smith, on his own initiative, said he would try to persuade Dulles to accept it.

On the afternoon of Thursday, March 12, Jackson drafted a letter to Dulles requesting definitive assurance that his conception of political warfare included a positive and even central role for the Department of State, calling to his attention the likelihood of a four-power meeting being forced upon the United States in the coming months, even if the proposed speech did not offer it.

Rostow returned to Cambridge on the night of March 12.

* * *

Post—March 12

Although I lack knowledge of the next stage in the process which led to the speech, I believe that the opening of the Soviet diplomatic peace offensive by Malenkov in his speech before the Supreme Soviet on March 16 resulted in a postponement of the speech as planned on Thursday, March 12. For the record it should be noted that Jackson and Rostow urged a prompt American initiative not only to exploit the psychological possibilities available immediately after Stalin's death but with an awareness that the new Soviet regime might seize the peace initiative. . . .

It is essential to an understanding of the conflict over this speech within the government that the relation of Jackson's initiative to EDC and Western European unity be distinguished from the view held generally in the Department of State (excepting Kennan and certain others). Both the Department of State and Jackson felt that a negotiation with the Soviet Union should take place, if at all possible, on the basis of EDC having been accomplished. In the Department of State, however, there was a deep unwillingness to contemplate such a negotiation unless it was forced upon us. In any case, it was felt in the Department that the United States should continue to use its influence directly—along familiar diplomatic lines—to bring about the completion of the EDC arrangement, as first priority, and to fend off as long as possible any four-power negotiation. It was Jackson's view that the chance of achieving EDC in the near future would be maximized if the United States were to take an initiative in the four-power negotiation and, within that framework, seek to induce our allies to go into the negotiation with the EDC arrangement behind us. It was feared by Jackson that, if the United States tried to evade a negotiation, that very fact would increase the difficulty of achieving EDC in the near future. Behind Jackson's position lay the following appreciation: that the unwillingness of many Germans to see EDC through hinged on their judgment that the

United States had no serious interest in German unity, and that a negotiation with the USSR was an alternative to EDC; and, similarly, that the unwillingness of many Frenchmen to see EDC through hinged on their judgment that the United States has no serious conception of a long-run German (and continental) settlement; that the United States might, therefore, step by step, turn continental hegemony over to the Germans; and that a negotiation with the USSR was an alternative to German rearmament, or might at least postpone it. Jackson's appreciation was not that a negotiation was likely to succeed, but, rather, that it might unite the Free World around a position which would make EDC a necessary and logical step, not negatively to oppose the USSR but positively to move towards a European settlement which would meet underlying American, German, French and other interests. At no point did the representatives of the Department of State appreciate this view or argue it; rather, they felt Jackson's initiative to be, simply, an uninformed gesture which failed to understand the key importance of EDC.

It was the fear of Jackson and Rostow that, without such a prompt U.S. initiative, that would bind up our support for EDC with a longer perspective on a European settlement, in any case EDC would be postponed until our allies had a chance to test the new Soviet regime's intentions.

Jackson's view on this matter was no new thing: the basic issue involved had been raised and fully discussed at the Princeton meeting of May 1952, and Jackson had obviously considered the problem posed by German and French attitudes to U.S. diplomatic objectives at an earlier time. Rostow's similar view was also of considerable vintage, stemming back to 1946, but articulated fully in the CENIS Soviet Vulnerability Report.

W. W. Rostow

May 11, 1953

Appendix D

State Department Memorandum with Consolidated Advice for the March 11, 1953, NSC Meeting

---

[*Note*: This memorandum contains the consolidated advice of State Department officials through the level of undersecretary of state for the March 11, 1953 NSC meeting. Only the passages on the proposed presidential statement and a negotiation with the Soviet Union are included. (From the C. D. Jackson Records, box 5, "Stalin's Death—PSB Plans for Exploitation of" folder, Dwight D. Eisenhower Library.)]

. . . the Department is opposed to a major Presidential speech at this time, as assumed in paragraph 3d. The initial shock of Stalin's death has produced for the time being unity and coherence in the regime. Significant opportunities to exploit Stalin's death by a speech are more likely to appear later on. The Department believes that the great power of a major Presidential speech should be reserved until an important opportunity arises and until it is clear how this opportunity can best be exploited. Meanwhile there are other actions which can be taken to exploit the present situation and which would not require a definite solution of a theme for a speech unrelated to the developing situation in the Soviet Union. The Department has the following specific comments about "an early high-level meeting (presumably between the Foreign Ministers of the U.S.S.R., Great Britain, France, and the U.S.A.) to consider certain outstanding issues."

a. A proposal for a Foreign Ministers' meeting presupposes that the United States will have specific matters to discuss and specific proposals to make. The U.S. should not commit itself to a meeting before such proposals have been formulated. To do otherwise might result in serious embarrassment to the President. If there are overriding reasons outside the field of foreign affairs for a Presidential speech at this time, the Department strongly recommends that the speech should not propose a meeting of Foreign Ministers or commit us to make specific proposals for the relaxation of international tensions.

b. The mere proposal for a Foreign Ministers' meeting without prior thorough consultation with our major allies, particularly the U.K. and France, would have a major divisive effect upon our relations with them. If it were decided to propose a meeting, the preparation of proposals and consultation with our allies would require some time. Without such consultation, the Soviet Union might be able to create sharp divisions within the Western coalition.

c. The Department believes that a meeting of Foreign Ministers would indefinitely delay progress on EDC. No action could be expected by European Governments on EDC pending outcome and evaluation of the Ministers' meeting. In the recent discussions with Mr. Eden, the Department has reaffirmed its intention to press for rapid progress on EDC.

d. The Department points out that the U.S. has always taken the position that Far Eastern problems are not within the competence of the Council of Foreign Ministers. The reason for this is that the CFM is subject to Soviet veto and that it is not in the interest of the U.S. to enable the Soviet Union to veto Far Eastern arrangements. The Department believes that this position should be maintained. It follows that if a meeting of Foreign Ministers is held, Far Eastern matters should be excluded. Moreover, the Department believes that a Korean armistice should be a precondition to efforts to settle other questions and therefore that other arrangements should be found for reaching a Korean armistice before a meeting of the CFM. It should be noted that any meeting on Far Eastern matters would raise serious questions of representation in the cases of Korea, Indochina, and China, especially on the principle that no arrangements affecting any country should be settled without participation by representatives of that country. . . .

Appendix E

The Full Text of Eisenhower's Speech of April 16 and Dulles' of April 18

[*Note*: This appendix includes the full text of Eisenhower's speech of April 16, 1953, and Dulles' speech of two days later, somewhat different in tone and emphasis. (From *Vital Speeches of the Day*, 19, no. 14, May 1, 1953, pp. 418–424.)]

PEACE IN THE WORLD
ACTS, NOT RHETORIC, NEEDED
By DWIGHT D. EISENHOWER, President of the United States
Delivered to the American Society of Newspaper Editors,
Washington, D.C.
April 16, 1953

President Bryan, distinguished guests of this association and ladies and gentlemen:

I am happy to be here.

I say this and I mean it very sincerely for a number of reasons. Not the least of these is the number of friends I am honored to count among you.

Over the years we have seen, talked, agreed and argued with one another on a vast variety of subjects under circumstances no less varied. We have met at home and in distant lands. We have been together at times when war seemed endless, at times when peace seemed near, at times when peace seemed to have eluded us again.

We have met in times of battle, both military and electoral, and all these occasions mean to me memories of enduring friendship.

I am happy to be here for another reason.

This occasion calls for my first formal address to the American people since assuming the office of the Presidency just twelve weeks ago. It is fitting, I think, that I speak to you, the editors of America.

You are in such a vital way both representatives of and responsible to the people of our country. In great part upon you, upon your intelligence, your integrity, your devotion to the ideals of freedom and justice themselves depend the understanding and the knowledge with which our people must meet the fact of twentieth century life.

Without such understanding and knowledge they would be incapable of promoting justice; without them they would be incapable of defending freedom.

Finally, I am happy to be here at this time before this audience because I must speak of that issue that comes first of all in the hearts and minds of all of us—that issue which most urgently challenges and summons the wisdom and the courage of our whole people.

This issue is peace.

In this spring of 1953 the free world weighs one question above all others: The chance for a just peace—just peace—for all peoples.

To weigh this chance is to summon instantly to mind another recent moment of great decision. It came with that yet more hopeful Spring of 1945, bright with the promise of victory and of freedom. The hope of all just men in that moment, too, was a just and lasting peace.

The eight years that have passed have seen that hope waver, grow dim, and almost die. And the shadow of fear again has darkly lengthened across the world.

Today the hope of free men remains stubborn and brave, but it is sternly disciplined by experience.

It shuns not only all crude counsel of despair, but also the self-deceit of easy illusion.

It weighs the chance for peace with sure, clear knowledge of what happened to the vain hope of 1945.

UNION AND DIVISION

In the spring of victory, the soldiers of the Western Alliance met the soldiers of Russia in the center of Europe. They were triumphant comrades in arms. Their peoples shared the joyous prospect of building, in honor of their dead, the only fitting monument—an age of just peace.

All these war-weary peoples shared, too, this concrete, decent purpose: To guard vigilantly against the domination ever again of any part of the world by a single, unbridled aggressive power.

This common purpose lasted an instant—and perished. The nations of the world divided to follow two distinct roads.

The United States and our valued friends, the other free nations, chose one road.

The leaders of the Soviet Union chose another.

The way chosen by the United States was plainly marked by a few clear precepts which govern its conduct in world affairs.

FIRST—No people on earth can be held—as a people—to be an enemy, for all humanity shares the common hunger for peace and fellowship and justice.

SECOND—No nation's security and well-being can be lastingly achieved in isolation, but only in effective cooperation with fellow-nations.

THIRD—Any nation's right to a form of government and an economic system of its own choosing is inalienable.

FOURTH—Any nation's attempt to dictate to other nations their form of government is indefensible.

AND FIFTH—A nation's hope of lasting peace cannot be firmly based upon any race in armaments, but rather upon just relations and honest understanding with all other nations.

THE WAY TO PEACE

In the light of these principles, the citizens of the United States defined the way they proposed to follow, through the aftermath of war, toward true peace.

This way was faithful to the spirit that inspired the United Nations: To prohibit strife, to relieve tensions, to banish fears. This way was to control and to reduce armaments. This way was to allow all nations to devote their energies and resources to the great and good tasks of healing the war's wounds, of clothing and feeding and housing the needy, of perfecting a just political life, of enjoying the fruits of their own free toil.

The Soviet Government held a vastly different vision of the future.

In the world of its design, security was to be found—not in mutual trust and mutual aid—but in force: Huge armies, subversion, rule of neighbor nations. The goal was power superiority—at all cost. Security was to be sought by denying it to all others.

The result has been tragic for the world and, for the Soviet Union, it has also been ironic.

The amassing of Soviet power alerted free nations to a new danger of aggression. It compelled them in self-defense to spend unprecedented money and energy for armaments. It forced them to develop weapons of war now capable of inflicting instant and terrible punishment on any aggressor.

It instilled in the free nations—and let none doubt this—the unshakable conviction that, as long as there persists a threat to freedom, they must, at any cost, remain armed, strong and ready for any risk of war.

It inspired them—and let none doubt this—to attain a unity of purpose and will beyond the power of propaganda or pressure to break, now or ever.

There remained, however, one thing essentially unchanged and unaffected by Soviet conduct: This unchanged thing was a readiness of the free world to welcome sincerely any genuine evidence of peaceful purpose enabling all peoples again to resume their common quest of just peace. And the free world still holds to that purpose.

The free nations, most solemnly and repeatedly, have assured the Soviet Union that their firm association has never had any aggressive purpose whatsoever.

Soviet leaders, however, have seemed to persuade themselves—or tried to persuade their people—otherwise.

And so it came to pass that the Soviet Union itself has shared and suffered the very fears it has fostered in the rest of the world.

This has been the way of life forged by eight years of fear and force.

116

What can the world—or any nation in it—hope for if no turning is found on this dread road?

The worst to be feared and the best to be expected can be simply stated.

The worst is atomic war.

The best would be this: A life of perpetual fear and tension; a burden of arms draining the wealth and the labor of all peoples; a wasting of strength that defies the American system or the Soviet system or any system to achieve true abundance and happiness for the peoples of this earth.

Every gun that is made, every warship launched, every rocket fired signifies—in the final sense—a theft from those who hunger and are not fed, those who are cold and are not clothed.

This world in arms is not spending money alone.

It is spending the sweat of its laborers, the genius of its scientists, the hopes of its children.

The cost of one modern heavy bomber is this: a modern brick school in more than 30 cities.

It is: Two electric power plants, each serving a town of 60,000 population.

It is: Two fine, fully equipped hospitals.

It is: Some 50 miles of concrete highway.

We pay for a single fighter plane with a half million bushels of wheat.

We pay for a single destroyer with new homes that could have housed more than 8,000 people.

NOT A WAY OF LIFE

This is—I repeat—the best way of life to be found on the road the world has been taking.

This is not a way of life at all, in any true sense. Under the cloud of threatening war, it is humanity hanging from a cross of iron.

These plain and cruel truths define the peril and point the hope that come with Spring of 1953.

This is one of those times in the affairs of nations when the gravest choices must be made—if there is to be a turning toward a just and lasting peace.

It is a moment that calls upon the governments of the world to speak their intentions with simplicity and with honesty.

It calls upon them to answer the question that stirs the hearts of all sane men: Is there no other way the world may live?

The world knows that an era ended with the death of Joseph Stalin. The extraordinary thirty-year span of his rule saw the Soviet empire expand to reach from the Baltic Sea to the Sea of Japan, finally to dominate 800,000,000 souls.

The Soviet system shaped by Stalin and his predecessors was born of one world war. It survived with stubborn and often amazing courage a second world war. It has lived to threaten a third.

NEW LEADERSHIP

Now a new leadership has assumed power in the Soviet Union. Its links to the past, however strong, cannot bind it completely. Its future is, in great part, its own to make.

This new leadership confronts a free world aroused, as rarely in its history, by the will to stay free.

This free world knows—out of bitter wisdom of experience—that vigilance and sacrifice are the price of liberty.

It knows that the peace and defense of Western Europe imperatively demands the unity of purpose and action made possible by the North Atlantic Treaty Organization, embracing a European Defense Community.

It knows that western Germany deserves to be a free and equal partner in this community; and that this, for Germany, is the only safe way to full, final unity.

It knows that aggression in Korea and in Southeast Asia are threats to the whole free community to be met by united action.

This is the kind of free world which the new Soviet leadership confronts. It is a world that demands and expects the fullest respect of its rights and interests. It is a world that will always accord the same respect to all others.

So the new Soviet leadership now has a precious opportunity to awaken, with the rest of the world, to a point of peril reached, and to help turn the tide of history.

Will it do this?

We do not yet know. Recent statements and gestures of Soviet leaders give some evidence that they may recognize this critical moment.

We welcome every honest act of peace.

We care nothing for mere rhetoric.

We care only for sincerity of peaceful purpose—attested by deeds. The opportunities for such deeds are many. The performance of a great number of them waits upon no complex protocol but upon the simple will to do them.

Even a few such clear and specific acts—such as the Soviet Union's signature upon an Austrian treaty, or its release of thousands of prisoners still held from World War II—would be impressive signs of sincere intent. They would carry a power of persuasion not to be matched by any amount of oratory.

This we do know: A world that begins to witness the rebirth of trust among nations can find its way to a peace that is neither partial nor punitive.

With all who will work in good faith toward such a peace, we are ready—with renewed resolve—to strive to redeem the near-lost hopes of our day.

The first great step along this way must be the conclusion of an honorable armistice in Korea.

This means the immediate cessation of hostilities and the prompt initiation of political discussions leading to the holding of free elections in a united Korea.

It should mean—no less importantly—an end to the direct and indirect attacks upon the security of Indo-China and Malaya. For any armistice in Korea that merely released aggressive armies to attack elsewhere would be a fraud.

We seek throughout Asia, as throughout the world, a peace that is true and total.

Out of this can grow a still wider task—the achieving of just political settlements for the other serious and specific issues between the free world and the Soviet Union.

None of these issues, great or small, is insoluble—given only the will to respect the rights of all nations.

Again we say: The United States is ready to assume its just part.

We have already done all within our power to speed conclusion of a treaty with Austria which will free that country from economic exploitation and from occupation by foreign troops.

We are ready not only to press forward with the present plans for closer unity of the nations of western Europe but also, upon that foundation, to strive to foster a broader European community, conducive to the free movement of persons, of trade, and of ideas.

This community would include a free and united Germany, with a government based upon free and secret ballot.

This free community and the full independence of the East European nations could mean the end of the present unnatural division of Europe.

As progress in all these areas strengthens world trust, we could proceed concurrently with the next great work—the reduction of the burden of armaments now weighing upon the world. To this end, we would welcome and enter into the most solemn agreements. These could properly include:

1. The limitation, by absolute numbers or by an agreed international ratio, of the sizes of the military and security forces of all nations.

2. A commitment by all nations to set an agreed limit upon that proportion of total production of certain strategic materials to be devoted to military purposes.

3. International control of atomic energy to promote its use for peaceful purposes only, and to ensure the prohibition of atomic weapons.

4. A limitation or prohibition of other categories of weapons of great destructiveness.

5. The enforcement of all these agreed limitations and prohibitions by adequate safeguards, including a practical system of inspection under the United Nations.

The details of such disarmament programs are manifestly critical and complex. Neither the United States nor any other nation can properly claim to possess a perfect, immutable formula. But the formula matters less than the faith—the good faith without which no formula can work justly and effectively.

A NEW KIND OF WAR

The fruit of success in all these tasks would present the world with the greatest task—and the greatest opportunity—of all. It is this: The dedication of the energies, the resources, and the imaginations of all peaceful nations to a new kind of war. This would be a declared, total war, not upon any human enemy, but upon the brute forces of poverty and need.

The peace we seek, founded upon decent trust and cooperative effort among nations, can be fortified—not by weapons of war—but by wheat and by cotton; by milk and by wool; by meat and by timber, and by rice.

These are words that translate into every language on earth.

These are needs that challenge this world in arms.

This idea of a just and peaceful world is not new or strange to us. It inspired the people of the United States to initiate the European Recovery Program in 1947. That program was prepared to treat, with equal concern, the needs of Eastern and Western Europe.

We are prepared to reaffirm, with the most concrete evidence, our readiness to help build a world in which all people can be productive and prosperous.

This Government is ready to ask its people to join with all nations in devoting a substantial percentage of any savings achieved by real disarmament to a fund for world aid and reconstruction. The purposes of this great work would be: To help other peoples to develop the underdeveloped areas of the world, to stimulate profitable and fair world trade, to assist all peoples to know the blessings of productive freedom.

The monuments to this new kind of war would be these: Roads and schools, hospitals and homes, food and health.

We are ready, in short, to dedicate our strength to serving the needs, rather than the fears, of the world.

I know of nothing I can add to make plainer the sincere purpose of the United States.

I know of no course, other than that marked by these and similar actions, that can be called the highway of peace.

I know of only one question upon which progress waits. It is this: What is the Soviet Union ready to do?

Whatever the answer may be, let it be plainly spoken.

Again we say: The hunger for peace is too great, the hour in history too late, for any government to mock men's hopes with mere words and promises and gestures.

Is the new leadership of the Soviet Union prepared to use its decisive influence in the Communist world—including control of the flow of arms—to bring not merely an expedient truce in Korea but genuine peace in Asia?

Is it prepared to allow other nations, including those of Eastern Europe, the free choice of their own forms of government?

Is it prepared to act in concert with others upon serious disarmament proposals?

If not—where then is the concrete evidence of the Soviet Union's concern for peace?

There is, before all peoples, a precious chance to turn the black tide of events.

If we failed to strive to seize this chance, the judgment of future ages would be harsh and just.

If we strive but fail, and the world remains armed against itself it at least need be divided no longer in its clear knowledge of who has condemned humankind to this fate.

The purpose of the United States, in stating these proposals, is simple and clear.

These proposals spring—without ulterior purpose or political passion—from our calm conviction that the hunger for just peace is in the hearts of all peoples—those of Russia and of China no less than of our own country.

They conform to our firm faith that God created men to enjoy, not destroy, the fruits of the earth and of their own toil.

They aspire to this: The lifting from the backs and from the hearts of men, of their burden of arms and of fears, so that they may find before them a golden age of freedom and of peace.

THE EISENHOWER FOREIGN POLICY
A WORLD-WIDE PEACE OFFENSIVE
By JOHN FOSTER DULLES, Secretary of State, United States
Delivered to the American Society of Newspaper Editors,
Washington, D.C.
April 18, 1953

President Eisenhower, speaking here last Thursday, opened the door to the mansion of peace. He invited the Soviet Union to come in. That invitation was not mere rhetoric. Its timing was not chosen at hazard. It marked a planned stage in the evolution of the Eisenhower foreign policy. The speech really had its beginning when President Eisenhower took office, which was ninety days ago tomorrow.

The words which President Eisenhower uttered might have been uttered at any time during these past ninety days. But these words gained immensely in significance because they come against a background of cohesive, positive action.

When President Eisenhower first took office, a plea for peace such as he made this week might have been interpreted as a sign of weakness or a mere gesture of sentimentality. In order that such a plea should carry maximum impact, it was first necessary to demonstrate to the world, and to Soviet leaders in particular, President Eisenhower's will and capacity to develop foreign policies so firm, so fair, so just, that the Soviet leaders might find it expedient to live with these policies rather than to live against them.

I should like briefly to review this ninety-day period, which had as its climax the President's historical address.

One of the worries of the free world, and one of the hopes of the Soviet world, has been disunity in Western Europe. For example, it would be particularly disastrous for the West if Franco-German antagonism were revived. That would indeed afford Soviet intrigue a fertile field of operation.

The Continental European countries themselves, including France and Germany, had seen the danger and had devised a program to meet it. They had proposed to create a European Defense Community, the members of which would merge their military power into a single force. A treaty to this effect was signed nearly a year ago. It was contemplated by the treaty that it would be ratified and come into force within six months. But, following the signatures of the treaty, nothing happened. Last January, it seemed that the project was dying.

The President, out of his own intimate knowledge of European conditions, felt that our Government should indicate its deep concern and point out that failure to realize the European Defense Community could mean collapse of the hopes and efforts that inspired the Marshall Plan, the North Atlantic Treaty and the Mutual Security Program. Therefore, on January 30, just ten days after the President's inaugural, Mr. Stassen and I, at the President's request, visited the six European Defense Community countries, and also Great Britain.

As a result of our visit, and the return visits to Washington of several European leaders, this project has now been revived. It cannot yet be confidently predicted that it will be realized. But it is today the liveliest single topic before the six Parliaments of Continental Europe.

The Soviet Union now faces the likelihood that Western Europe will produce a unified military force, including French and Germans. Thus would come to a final end one of the hopes from which Soviet imperialism has taken comfort.

It was never expected that the European Defense Community, when created, would alone carry the burdens of making Western Europe secure. EDC, a community of six, would stand within the framework of NATO, a partnership of fourteen. This partnership, however, also presented us with urgent problems. For most of the members had come to feel that the program for NATO represented a type of effort which they could not continue indefinitely to bear.

The United States and its NATO partners had been operating on the assumption that the moment of greatest danger was some early, predictable date. Therefore, it had been reasoned, emergency efforts should be made to meet that date, leaving subsequent years for stabilization and recuperation.

But the Soviet Union did not conveniently relax its threat in order to meet the preconceived timetable of the NATO countries. Accordingly, it was found necessary each year to prolong the extraordinary exertion and to defer the period of stabilization. This spasmodic approach was exhaustive to all concerned. Several of our Allies told us that they could not hold the present pace without greatly increased help from the United States.

The situation obviously called for a fresh approach.

Because we did not believe that any specific date of peak danger could be reliably forecast; because Soviet communism itself professes to operate in terms of "an entire historical era"; because new weapons inevitably change the aspect of the military task; because a vigorous and happy society is itself an important ingredient of freedom—for these reasons we decided to find programs which, on the one hand, will provide Europe with substantial insurance against being overrun by Soviet attack, and which, on the other hand, can, if necessary, be sustained for an indefinite period with growing reliance on Western Europe's own strength.

Next week the Secretary of the Treasury, Mr. Humphrey; the Secretary of Defense, Mr. Wilson; the Director for Mutual Security, Mr. Stassen, and I will go to Paris to meet with the other members of the North Atlantic Treaty Organization Council. There we shall listen sympathetically to the point of view of our partners and together with them concert military programs designed to deter attack from without, without undermining inner strength.

All will know, and I am confident that the Soviet leaders know best of all, that what we plan is not greater weakness but greater strength. The productivity of the free world is so prodigious, its inventiveness so phenomenal, that a military aggressor that attacked our free world partnership would be doomed to sure defeat.

What we plan is to dissipate another Soviet hope, the hope expressed by Stalin when he said that "the moment for the decisive blow" would come when the opponents of communism "have sufficiently weakened themselves in a struggle which is beyond their strength." We do not intend that that moment of bankruptcy shall come.

Let me add that the policy here expressed was determined upon without regard to any of the recent Soviet moves. We are not dancing to any Russian tune. Nothing that has happened has induced in us a mood of relaxation or any desire to weaken NATO. The purpose and the result will be a NATO more sure to live and to perform its appointed tasks.

In the Far East, vigorous policy decisions were also taken since the ninety days began. In Korea we embarked upon a program to change the complexion of that struggle. As President Eisenhower told you, we still welcome an armistice, not merely to end the fighting but on the assumption that it will lead to a peace which accords with the principles of the United Nations—and that means a free and united Korea. Of course we want peace in Korea. But we do not play the role of suppliants.

We have vastly improved our relations with the national Government of China. We now have an Ambassador at Taipei, Formosa, the provisional capital. We are speeding delivery of military assistance which was woefully in arrears. President Eisenhower has changed the instructions to the Seventh Fleet so that, while it is still instructed to protect Formosa, it is no longer instructed to protect the Chinese Communists on the mainland.

In relation to Indo-China, the French Government and the Associated States have been told that we would be favorably disposed to giving increased military and financial assistance to plans realistically designed to suppress the Communist-inspired civil war which for six years has wracked the area and seriously drained the metropolitan resources of France.

We recently announced, in conjunction with the French Government, that should the Chinese Communist regime take advantage of a Korean armistice to pursue aggressive war elsewhere in the Far East, such action would have the most serious consequences and would conflict directly with the understanding on which any armistice in Korea was reached. That decision was taken prior to the recent revival of prospects for Korean armistice. It was part of our efforts to anticipate what may happen rather than to catch up with what has happened.

We negotiated with the Governments of Britain, France and other maritime powers for tightening of the blockade of Communist China. They are taking important practical measures to restrict the voyages of their own ships to China and to withhold the fuel from ships of other nations which are carrying strategic goods to China.

You can see, as others have seen, that a new order of priority and urgency has been given to the Far East. Further, it has been made clear that we consider that our Far Eastern friends, from Japan, Korea and Formosa, to Indo-China and Malaya, face a single hostile front, to be met with a common purpose and growing cooperation as between the component parts of freedom.

This means that the Communists in the Far East can no longer count on winning by shifting their strength and by focusing their attacks on one or another free world position that is isolated from the others. The Communist strategy, based on a contiguous land mass, is now confronted by a growing free world unity based upon the peninsular positions and offshore island chains now controlled by the free peoples of Asia.

The Middle East and Latin America, two areas far apart, have both been the subject of Communist attempts at infiltration. The ground was fertile because these areas have somewhat lacked our attention, and, in the case of the Middle East, there has developed a spirit of nationalism, which has at times grown fanatical in its opposition to the Western Powers.

As was announced some weeks ago, Mr. Stassen and I have been invited by the Governments of more than a dozen countries of the Middle East and South Asia to visit them. We have accepted and plan to go next month. That is significant, for no United States Secretary of State has ever visited any of these countries. It will afford us opportunity to meet at first hand many of the leaders and, I hope, to dissipate the false impression which Communist propaganda has fomented.

As President Eisenhower announced last Sunday, the State Department is organizing a goodwill mission to South America which will be headed by the President's brother, Dr. Milton Eisenhower. He will personally carry the President's sentiments of good will toward the republics and people to the south of us. Our new Assistant Secretary for this area is already in Central America.

I have had the pleasure of two meetings, one of the United Nations and the other at Washington, with the representatives of all twenty of the American republics.

What we have done, and what we already planned, mark a determination to develop better understanding and more fellowship, with people whom we know and respect, but whose friendship we have taken too much for granted. Thereby, we may close another possible avenue of Soviet Communist aggression.

The free peoples are susceptible to Soviet guile because they so passionately want peace that they can readily be attracted by illusions of peace. One such illusion is a settlement based on the status quo. This present status involves the captivity of hundreds of millions of persons of distinctive nationality, race, religion and culture. The hardest task of the Soviet rulers is to beat this disunity into Communist conformity. If that can be done, then the menace of Soviet communism will be immeasurably increased.

It was of the utmost importance that we should make clear to the captive people that we do not accept their captivity as a permanent fact of history. If they thought otherwise and became hopeless, we would unwittingly have become partners to the forging of a hostile power so vast that it would encompass our destruction.

President Eisenhower, anticipating some of the events that have since occurred, acted immediately after his inauguration to propose that our national position should be made clear through a solemn resolution concurred in by Congress and the President. The Congress has yet to act. However, I am persuaded, and I trust that the captive peoples are persuaded, that Congress in fact fully shares the point of view that President Eisenhower expressed. In any event, the Chief Executive has formulated his position on this important matter, and by doing so has foreclosed another of the hopes which Soviet rulers have optimistically entertained.

While we have been making these policy decisions, we have at the same time been acting to assure that the State Department would be able to make new policies wherever these would seem better than the old and to assure a steadily rising level of performance.

In addition to the new Secretary of State, there are two new Under Secretaries, one of whom specializes in administration and security matters. There are six new Assistant Secretaries. There is a new legal adviser, a new counselor, a new director of the International Information Administration, who has responsibility for the Voice of America. The whole Policy Planning Staff is to go under new directions and be coordinated closely with the revitalized National Security Council.

We are also bringing a fresh vision and new vigor into our United Nations mission and into our embassies abroad. The chief of the permanent mission to the United Nations, former Senator Austin, retired last January after many years of distinguished service. He has been succeeded by former Senator Henry Cabot Lodge, who now heads the permanent mission. His vigor and parliamentary skill already demonstrate that the Soviet leaders cannot look forward to using the United Nations as a sounding board for propaganda, but that they will have to deal in the United Nations with a mobilized body of world opinion which is determined that the United Nations shall, in fact, serve its avowed purpose to maintain international peace and security in conformity with the principles of justice.

FOREIGN SERVICE AIDES

New ambassadors are installed or being installed in Great Britain, Ireland, France, Italy, Germany, Russia, Spain, Mexico, Brazil, Japan, free China, India and Pakistan. Other appointments are in contemplation.

For the first time in State Department history all our major appointments are subject to F.B.I. field checks so as to eliminate security risks and possibility of hostile infiltration into high places. So far as is humanly practical, we are seeing to it that Communist agents cannot have access to the State Department.

We are fortunate in having a body of Foreign Service career men and women who can be the main reliance of the President and myself. They are a permanent and nonpolitical part of Government. They became such under the Rogers Act, enacted by a Republican Congress during the Administration of President Coolidge and Secretary Hughes.

There is a tendency in some quarters to feel that confidence cannot be placed in these career officials because in the past, as was their duty, they served under Democrat Presidents and Secretaries of State. It is, however, easier than most think for former career Foreign Service men and women to adapt themselves to new Republican leadership. Like career soldiers, Foreign Service officers respect and welcome high policy direction such as they are getting under President Eisenhower. They are, with rare exception, a splendid and patriotic group of men and women, with a fine tradition. They are experts, trained to analyze and interpret foreign conditions and to carry out designated missions, usually of delicacy, sometimes of danger. Just as the nation depends, for defense purposes, on the graduates of our military and naval academies, so the nation, for foreign services, depends on our career diplomats.

Our people here at home, our friends abroad and our enemies abroad know that we have not only strong foreign policies but that we are rapidly molding an organization which will be secure and which will be efficient in action.

I might add as of particular interest to this distinguished group of American editors that these foreign policies of which I speak are no longer looked upon as state secrets. We are determined that the public shall be as fully informed as possible, and in the clearest and simplest language possible, about what we are doing in the State Department and what our foreign policy is.

I have long felt that, under our form of government, the effectiveness of foreign policy depends in large measure upon public understanding and support of it.

Our conduct has been calmly strong, never truculent nor blustering. In the face of it, Soviet leaders gave evidence that they were changing their policies. They initiated what presents to you and to me one of the most perplexing problems of our times. It is a problem that I think is largely due to a misnomer. The Kremlin launched what is commonly called a "peace offensive." Whatever it is that the Kremlin has launched—and no one can be sure just yet what it is—it is not a peace *offensive*. It is a peace *defensive*.

BASIC CHANGE

It is gratifying that Soviet leaders appear now to have shifted from an offensive to a defensive mood. But we cannot yet tell whether this represents a basic change or merely a tactical shift. It is prudent, for the present, to assume that we are witnessing a tactical move of the kind which Soviet communism has often practiced.

Stalin, in his classic treatise on "Strategy and Tactics," taught that, from time to time, "concessions" may have to be made "in order to buy off a powerful enemy and gain a respite." He went on to explain the necessity of maneuvering with a "view to effecting a proper retreat when the enemy is strong. The object of this strategy is to gain time and to accumulate forces in order later to assume the offensive."

Is the successor—or shall I say, are the successors—following this strategy of the dead Stalin?

Whatever the reason and purpose of present Soviet moves, the fact is that the Communist leaders seem now disposed to grant some things which they formerly denied.

Last February 22, in an effort to probe the mood of the enemy in Korea, we quietly proposed an exchange of sick and wounded prisoners of war. Such proposals had frequently been made before, without results. This time a result seems to be in the making.

I should perhaps explain, to end some misunderstanding, that while under the agreement made we will return many more sick and wounded prisoners than we will receive, that is because the total number of prisoners which we hold is many times the number held by the Communists. The ratio of returning sick and wounded to the total prisoners of war held is approximately the same for both sides, with a slight advantage in our favor.

It also now appears that the enemy may now want an armistice in Korea, after having evaded it for nearly two years.

In other respects and in other quarters Communist leadership is making concessions. These are all still minor, but not without significance. They suggested to us that the time had come to launch a true peace offensive. That, President Eisenhower has done. Soviet leadership is now confronted by the Eisenhower tests. Will it meet, one by one, the issues with which President Eisenhower has challenged it? If so, will it abolish and abandon, in fact as well as in name, the Cominform through which it endlessly conspires to overthrow from within, every genuinely free Government in the world? We await the deeds which will give answer to these questions. We profoundly hope that these deeds will, in fact, end a black chapter of distrust and open a bright new chapter of peace and goodwill.

Some weeks ago when I was at the United Nations, I said the Stalin era had ended and the Eisenhower era had begun, bringing with it new hope for all mankind. Already that prediction is in process of confirmation. President Eisenhower's address is a fact which will inevitably influence the course of history. Around the world peoples and Governments have universally welcomed that address. In all the capitals of the free world, press and radio have demonstrated an unprecedented, spontaneous support for the President's call for a world-wide peace offensive and his challenge to the new Soviet leadership to back up their words with deeds. That response is not merely because of the words the President used, but because what he said had its setting in a ninety-day framework.

I do not attempt to read the future. That must always remain obscure so long as vast power is possessed by men who accept no guidance from the moral law. But surely our duty is clear. Those who represent a nation with the tradition and power of the United States must act boldly and strongly for what they believe to be right. The future is for a higher verdict.

Appendix F

Dulles Accepts the Speech

[*Note*: Dulles, while still identifying problems, accepts the concept of the presidential speech. (From the John Foster Dulles Papers, Presidential Speech Series, box 1, "President's Speech, April 1953" folder 2, Dwight D. Eisenhower Library.)]

April 6, 1953

MEMORANDUM FOR THE PRESIDENT

Subject: "Chance of Peace" Speech

1. I enclose redraft which, I trust, preserves the original impact while avoiding most of the political pitfalls.

2. The text on military matters should take account of Defense comments. I am sending Mr. Wilson a copy of this draft.

3. The U.K. and French Ambassadors should be promptly informed of the prospective speech and given an oral outline of its *substantive* aspects. The German sentences should be checked with Adenauer.

4. It should be recognized that peace in Asia will raise very difficult problems, abroad, and domestically, regarding the status of Formosa and the ambitions of the Nationalists there.

5. It should also be recognized that the speech may slightly augment the tendency to slow down E.D.C. or NATO plans (doubtless a Soviet prime objective). But these plans have always been vulnerable to a serious Soviet "peace" offensive.

6. The final tone of the speech should take account of intervening events, notably the progress on exchanging sick and wounded P.W.'s.

John Foster Dulles

Appendix G

The Final Draft of the Princeton Statement of U.S. Foreign Policy Goals, May 11, 1952

[*Note*: The final draft of the Princeton statement of U.S. foreign policy goals, dated May 11, 1952, foreshadows to a degree the approach taken by C. D. Jackson and me to the first draft of the statement for Eisenhower in the wake of Stalin's death.]

American foreign policy seeks three related goals: the defense of the United States; the creation and maintenance of a structure of world peace in accordance with the Charter of the United Nations; the development of conditions in which peoples may freely establish the governments and institutions under which they live.

In the war against Nazism the United States and the United Kingdom, as well as the Soviet Union, pledged themselves to the principle that the countries liberated from Nazi despotism should enjoy the right to governments and institutions of their own choice. The Soviet Union has, in fact, repudiated this pledge and ruthlessly prevented the peoples of Central and Eastern Europe from exercising this right.

We share with these countries the common interest that no single power shall again dominate Europe, destroying their national existence and threatening our own. It follows therefore that it is a basic tenet of American policy that liberty shall be restored to these countries within a framework of organization which will sustain the peace.

It is our faith and purpose that these goals be achieved without resort to war.

To this end we propose:

To continue to strive, together with the countries of Western Europe, for the establishment of a Europe united for economic welfare and common security.

To envisage the entrance of the countries of Central and Eastern Europe now under Soviet domination as equal members in this family of friendly nations, as soon as their national liberties are restored.

To strive for a democratic unification of Germany in order that a Germany thus unified may become a constructive member of the European family with security that it may never again be a threat to East or West.

To link these objectives to continuing efforts to achieve an effective world-wide armament reduction and control for which they would constitute a powerful support.

Armament is a temporary shield necessary to hold an aggressor in check. It is not a lasting solution to the desire of all people to live in peace and freedom and to devote their energies and resources to human welfare according to the dictates of their spiritual values.

It is the evident lesson of this century that men cannot live in peace and freedom when Europe is threatened by the domination of a single power. No nation can achieve security in Europe or elsewhere unilaterally. With effective world-wide security arrangements our objectives in no way threaten the Russian national interest. On the contrary, they would afford the Russian peoples a security now denied them by the unilateral and imperialist policies of the Soviet regime and they would permit the vast resources of Russia to be used for the welfare of the Russian peoples.

The stated goal of this declaration is freedom and peace for the peoples of many lands. The United States has no intention of imposing its cultural, social, economic or political patterns on any country. It respects the spiritual and cultural traditions of each nation as that nation's priceless heritage. It recognizes that each nation must be free to organize the forms of its national life, limited only by the common requirements of European and world peace, so that the deep spiritual, social and economic aspirations of men will find progressive fulfillment.

Appendix H

Stalin's Responses to James Reston's Four Questions of December 18, 1952, as Published December 25

[*Note*: On December 18, 1952, James Reston submitted four questions to Stalin through the Soviet ambassador to the United States, Georgi Zarubin. Stalin's responses were received from Zarubin late on the twenty-fourth in time for the Christmas edition of the *New York Times*.]

Herewith are the replies of Premier J. V. Stalin to the questions you asked him in your letter of Dec. 18, 1952, addressed to me [Zarubin].

Q.—At the beginning of a new year and a new Administration in the United States, is it still your conviction that the Union of Soviet Socialist Republics and the United States can live peacefully in the coming years?

A.—I still believe that war between the United States of America and the Soviet Union cannot be considered inevitable, and that our countries can continue to live in peace.

Q.—Wherein lie the sources of present world contention, in your judgment?

A.—Everywhere and in everything wherever the aggressive actions of the policy of the "cold war" against the Soviet Union find their expression.

Q.—Would you welcome diplomatic conversations with representatives of the new Eisenhower Administration looking toward the possibility of a meeting between yourself and General Eisenhower on easing world tensions?

A.—I regard this suggestion favorably.

Q.—Would you cooperate in any new diplomatic approach designed to bring about an end to the Korean war?

A.—I agree to cooperate because the U.S.S.R. is interested in ending the war in Korea.

Appendix I

Dulles to Hughes Memorandum of April 10, 1953

[*Note*: Dulles wrote this memorandum to Hughes on April 10, 1953, just before the former's departure on vacation, when the speech draft was nearing final form. This was the secretary of state's final intervention before the speech was delivered. (From the John Foster Dulles Papers, Presidential Speech Series, box 1, "Preisdent's Speech, April 1953" folder 3, Dwight D. Eisenhower Library.)]

With reference to the draft of the President's speech which you gave me this morning I have the following comments.

The references on pages 7, 8, and 11 to ending of wars in Asia give me a little concern lest it commit us to end the Chinese Civil war and again to "neutralize" Formosa.

I have pencilled in some suggestions designed to limit our proposal to Korea and Indochina, leaving out what might be interpreted as referring to China.

I believe that the questions on page 11 should reintroduce Austria, which is, I believe, next to Korea the clearest test of Soviet intentions which we should welcome. I suggest a new paragraph, reading: "Is it prepared to give Austria its freedom?"

Also there could be introduced at this point a reference to the German and Japanese war prisoners. Chancellor Adenauer particularly asked for this and the President indicated a sympathetic reception to his proposal. This would also bring in something which would be very effective in Japan, which otherwise is ignored in the speech. I suggest this: "Is it prepared to assuage the great grief by allowing the tens of thousands of German and Japanese military and civilian exiles from World War II to return to their homes?"

J.F.D.

N.B.—The pencilled suggestions are on the draft which the Secretary has with him.

cc: Mr. Nitze—who has copy of the speech (per Mr. Hughes)

Appendix J

Nitze Still Resistant, March 1953

[*Note*: This appendix includes Paul Nitze's memorandum to the secretary of state on the March 19 draft of the president's speech. (From the John Foster Dulles Papers, Presidential Speech Series, box 1, "President's Speech, April 1953" folder 3, Dwight D. Eisenhower Library.)]

"PEACE PLAN SPEECH"
Considerations relating to the redraft of
March 19, 1953

1. If the plan for peace outlined in the March 19 draft is advanced, it seems clear that the Soviet Union would not at this time be prepared to accept the principles enunciated by the President. It is not so clear, however, that the Soviet Union would reject the proposals outright. There is a strong possibility that the Kremlin might ask for a meeting in order to secure a clarification.

2. It should be recognized that, after advancing the proposals, it would be difficult for the President to oppose a meeting if one were requested by the Kremlin. It should also be recognized that the Kremlin would attempt to use any meeting as a propaganda weapon, at least to delay and complicate the passage of the EDC Treaty. The countries of Western Europe would probably not be willing to go forward with the EDC as long as discussions of a general plan for peace were in progress.

3. Since the Soviet reaction is unpredictable, the plan for peace should also be considered in the context of an outright Soviet rejection. In this context, it does not appear that the interest of the

United States would be damaged, although there would probably be considerable comment to the effect that there was very little new in the plan and therefore that it amounted largely to a propaganda move.

4. Probably the only element of the plan that would cause an undesirable consequence in Western Europe is the fifth point relating to the withdrawal of American forces. The Europeans are very sensitive to such an idea and they might consider that the speech indicated the United States was considering this matter even in the absence of the acceptance of the terms of a plan for peace. This danger can be somewhat reduced by the revision of the language on page 6.

5. There is some question whether it is desirable to refer to a "four year" plan for peace. Putting a time period on the plan seems to have no particular relation to the elements to the plan itself, and the phrase "four year plan" might carry the unfortunate connotation of the Soviet "five year plan." It also seems unnecessary to suggest the carrying-out of the Plan will require four years. Perhaps an alternative would be a "Five Point Plan for Peace."

6. There are attached some suggested specific revisions of the language of the March 19th redraft for consideration. [Not included here.]

7. In view of the fact that we could not alone carry out the concrete proposals and the fact that the proposals would be of direct concern to our major allies (particularly the U.K. and France), it would be extremely harmful to our relations if this Plan for Peace were made public without prior consultation.

Appendix K

Three Rostow-Jackson Letters, April 1953

[*Note*: These letters from the author to C. D. Jackson were written at two points (April 1 and April 8) in the evolution of the draft of Eisenhower's April 16 speech. The last letter was written immediately after its delivery (April 17).]

April 1, 1953

Dear C.D.:

On returning to Cambridge, I swore a solemn oath that, having had a rare chance to say my piece in Washington, I would withhold further invaluable advice until asked. The last few days' news, however, has stirred me up again. So, here goes.

It seems to me that the latest element in the Russian peace offensive—the suggestion about a negotiation for a German peace treaty—has brought about, at Russian initiative, exactly what was feared by the State Department in connection with our proposal. That is, France and Germany are unlikely to proceed with EDC until after we have had a thorough exploration of what all this cooing of doves means.

In the face of this Soviet initiative we can do one of three things: (1) we can continue to beg the European governments to go ahead with EDC, on the grounds that the Russians don't mean business; (2) we can postpone EDC until after we have explored how far they are ready to go, and on what terms; or (3) we can urge them to go ahead with EDC in terms of a new positive Western position. It is the third position, which is essentially the one we took at the beginning of all this, which I think should not be excluded from deliberations in Washington.

Specifically, it requires that we ourselves recognize, and that we get our allies to recognize, that it is most unlikely that the Russians will give away anything important with respect to Eastern Germany unless they are convinced that we are capable of going ahead with Western German rearmament, should they not agree. The chance of achieving what we and our allies would like, if it is at all a real chance, doesn't only depend on the Russians, it depends on whether the West as a whole presents a common determined front. We cannot present such a front unless the Germans *really* believe that we want German unity; and unless the French *really* believe that our long-run vision of Europe is sufficiently well thought through so that we would not turn Europe back to the Germans in a fit of absent-mindedness.

What I am saying is that the "reversal of the wheel" that we talked about with Kennan still must take place. More than that, it should take place before a major conference, unless we are to go into it still at the mercy of initiatives from Moscow, still running the danger that they might separate us from the Western Germans and/or the French at the conference table.

Specifically, what this involves is: (1) our making up our minds and saying most solemnly in public that, if Korea is settled, we intend to seek the control of armaments and a unified Germany in a unified Europe (including Eastern Europe); (2) our carrying out swiftly, with the French and Western Germans especially but also with the British, some first-class diplomacy designed to convince them that the way to go to the conference table is with the EDC arrangements behind us, which they will only do if they really believe that this administration, as opposed to the last administration, is out to end the split of Germany and Europe by diplomacy, if possible, and, if not, by all means short of war; (3) our trying to bring Adenauer and the Social Democrats in Germany together on this position, perhaps by sending George Kennan over, as a special emissary on this matter, to help [James Bryant] Conant.

Whatever is decided upon, we must be aware of the two basic weaknesses thus far in our position: First, we have let Moscow call the tune and define the issues before the world. We have acted as if it were up to them to decide to what extent and on what matters of substance the Cold War can be diminished or liquidated. This is very dangerous. Without a clear picture of what we want, we run the risk of seeing the Free World split by the Soviet peace offensive, or of being dragged, like a reluctant dragon, to the council tables. Second, as near as I can make out, the State Department has not solved the problem of simultaneously advocating a united Germany in a united Europe while pressing for the measures of Western unification, which are absolutely essential until that goal is attained.

I thus come round to the view that a Presidential speech is still required, much more nearly like the one you showed to the PSB on Thursday, March 12, than the one Marie showed me the other day.

My deepest feelings about the present situation are that we may not exploit its possibilities to the full limit of America's power. I find some of the gestures of the Soviet peace offensive quite impressive. By that I mean I think they mean business, up to a point. The odds are that that point goes no further than the ending of the Korean War and a more stable accommodation to the split down the middle of Europe. Of course, we wish to see the Korean War ended on proper terms. But this isn't enough. If we are to push them further towards a real solution, we must convince them that we are dead serious about German rearmament, unless they do go further. If we are to convince them about German rearmament, we must hold the Western alliance together in the face of this peace offensive. I don't believe this, in turn, can be done unless the Germans believe we have the vision of an organization of the European continent as a whole which would effectively exclude the possibilities of German domination. Our attitude of "don't trouble your little heads about these matters, just get on with EDC" has failed to keep us really together; and I believe it will continue to fail.

Forgive this filibuster; but these are very important days in our history, and there is a danger that the burden of day-to-day jobs may keep us from doing the right thing. I have a picture of what the right things are. I am not by any means sure that my view is correct. I am sure that it should be among the alternatives examined.

All the best.

Yours,
W. W. Rostow

Dear C.D.,

On reflection, the new piece of paper is much better than the previous one, and someone is to be congratulated.

To make it as good as it can be, I suggest the following: that you and Emmet Hughes hie yourselves off to some place where there are no telephones, a bottle of bourbon, and about six consecutive hours; and that you check off every phrase, as well as the speech as a whole, against the following questions—

1. Will this unite our country and make it easier to push on with an adequate security program?

2. Will it heighten Free World unity in general?

3. Will it convince the French that, in advocating German unity, we do not intend to turn Europe over to Germany in a fit of absent-mindedness?

4. Will it convince the Germans that we really want German unity, in our own interest?

5. Will it convince the Germans that we will not negotiate over their heads with the Russians without full consultation with them?

6. Will it convince the East Europeans that we wish to draw them into a Europe which is not German-dominated?

7. Will it convince the Russian military that, in seeking an all-European organization, we are prepared to consider sympathetically their legitimate national security interests?

8. Will it convince the underdeveloped areas that our concern with their problems is long-run in character and transcends even the possibility of some kind of tempering of the Cold War with the Russians?

9. In general, does it present our NATO and other Free World plans as a constructive stage towards the sort of world we want, or does it continue to present them as a defensive reaction against Russian aggression which will have to be scrapped in the face of agreement?

10. Does it recognize that the aspirations of men are not merely material but fundamentally concerned with the achievement of greater human dignity?

My impression is that most of these elements are in the draft. But, as you are aware, this speech is awaited with a peculiarly acute thirst. It will be read with the utmost care by friend and foe and sceptic. A last 10% effort at refinement will be well worth while.

Beyond this, J.F.D. and Cabot Lodge, as well as our representatives all over the place, must be absolutely prepared to answer the searching technical diplomatic questions that will immediately be asked. Above all, they must be prepared to explain why it is that, although we honestly seek a German settlement, we believe a prior agreement on EDC will increase the chances of a serious settlement, not foreclose them.

All the best.

Yours,
W. W. Rostow

April 17, 1953

Dear C.D.,

Here, for what they may be worth, are some reflections after reading the morning's newspapers and getting the reaction to the President's speech of a reasonable sample of people hereabouts.

1. In terms of technical diplomacy, note above all the German reaction. Nothing we have done has brought the Social Democrats and Adenauer's government closer together. If we persist with EDC as a stage towards German unity—really meaning it about unity— we have a chance of holding the show together. To maintain momentum, however, not only Dulles but the Department of State must really back the play.

2. In the diplomatic follow-up, it may be more necessary, than in the speech itself, to clarify American intent that it ultimately unify Germany without creating a' threat. This is important for RFE and political warfare to Eastern Europe as well as for France.

3. These and other refinements of our long-run position may be judged academic by some since on all the evidence available it seems most unlikely that the Soviet Union will now cave in on Eastern Germany. What such "realists" must appreciate—and you have a perfect right to drive it home to them—is that a negotiation on Germany is likely to raise these key issues of potential dissension among our friends, and that it will be necessary to have formulae which cover them, if we are to emerge from a negotiation that fails, with a united Free World.

4. In the broadest sense, what the President's speech has done is

to bring into play the major constructive strengths of American and Free World political life for almost the first time since January 20. The job now is to keep them in play. You must appreciate that there is a marked contrast between the mood and substance of the President's speech on the one hand and the day-to-day performance of the government over the past weeks on such issues as:

—tariffs and British electrical equipment;

—Dulles on the Fourth Point;

—Stassen and McCarthy.

I think you have gotten the coal out of the bathtubs just fine, old boy, and I know you can't free Mooney and Billings right away;* but, nevertheless, there is a general political dynamics to an initiative of this kind which ought to be exploited. In particular, Dulles and Stassen ought to take heart and not merely write follow-up speeches but generate the staff work to back up the President's lead and act within the orbit of the confident and wise lines of foreign policy laid down. There is, of course, a real and living struggle between American idealism and the requirements of Free World leadership on the one hand and taxes on the other. This will remain with us. But the President's speech should bring the conflict into a bit better balance, if it is properly followed up.

In the midst of all this I have thought fondly of the Princeton meeting and hope, now, that the RFE boys can really build the new structure of themes they so badly needed last May.

On reflection, your shield is in the right place—and you're not on it.

Yours,
W. W. Rostow

---

*The reference here is to an old story Jackson and I shared about a rent strike in the Bronx. After being picketed by tenants carrying a variety of signs, the landlord assembled the tenants and said: "All right, I'll get the rat exterminator in; I'll get the coal out of the bathtubs; I'll put lights on the staircase; but how the hell can I free Mooney and Billings?"

Appendix L

*Jackson's Letter to Dulles Following
the April 16 Speech*

[*Note*: In this letter to Dulles, C. D. Jackson returns to the issue of a
negotiation with the Soviet Union and its relation to EDC promptly in the
wake of the April 16 speech. (From the C. D. Jackson Records, box 2,
"John Foster Dulles" folder, Dwight D. Eisenhower Library.)]

April 16, 1953

Dear Foster:

The heaviest burden of implementing the President's Message to
the Kremlin will inevitably fall upon you and your diplomatic arm.
Needless to say, you have a terrible problem in connection with the
Korean armistice—not to mention EDC and/or the possibility of the
Russians asking for a Four Power Conference on German unifica-
tion or anything else they might think of.

I hope, as soon as the Kremlin gives any indication of reacting to
the President's Message, that you will want to make a public appearance, television or radio, in order quickly to counter and press
forward.

It seems to me that if they show any indication of reaching for
any of the easier carrots that have been dangled, our tactic should
be to keep up the pressure before the world by tying in each
forward step with the next one which we will say must be taken by
the Russians.

Two or three times within the last fortnight, Beedle Smith has thought out loud about the possibility of events occurring which might make it advisable for us to take the initiative in calling for a Four Power Conference—in other words, quite a reversal of the position of several weeks ago. I am sure that you have already thought of the advisability of advance planning for such an eventuality.

Another thought in this connection which has doubtless occurred to you is that by skillful and forceful diplomatic moves in Western Europe, EDC could be sold as an essential prerequisite for a successful Four Power Conference, instead of allowing the impression to prevail that the suggestion of a Four Power Conference is the death knell of EDC.

Good luck and strength to your arm in Paris.

Sincerely yours,
C. D. Jackson

Honorable John Foster Dulles
The Secretary of State
Washington, D.C.
bc—Governor Harold E. Stassen
CDJ/mm/ekm

Appendix M

The Speech Viewed from Moscow

[*Note*: This appendix includes the Soviet commentary on Eisenhower's April 16 speech as well as Ambassador Bohlen's analysis of it. (The Soviet material is from *The Current Digest of the Soviet Press* 5, no. 14, May 16, 1953, pp. 5–8. Bohlen's analysis is from the White House Central Files, Confidential Series, box 61, "Russia—Stalin's Death and Reaction" folder 5, Dwight D. Eisenhower Library.)]

(Editorial)—ON PRESIDENT EISENHOWER'S SPEECH.

(Pravda and Izvestia, April 25, p. 1. Complete text:) Eight years have passed since the victory of the Allies—the U.S.S.R., the U.S.A., Britain and France—over Hitlerite fascism and the end of the second world war. The Soviet people bore the main burden of the great struggle. They did this to defend the freedom and independence of their fatherland, to help liberate the enslaved peoples of Europe from the fascist yoke and to secure a lasting peace and international security after the end of the war.

Steadfastly defending the cause of peace among peoples, the Soviet Union, as it has before, is striving for the development of international cooperation. The speeches by Comrades M. Malenkov, L. P. Beria and V. M. Molotov on March 9, 1953, express the inflexible will of the Soviet people to strengthen universal peace.

On April 16 U.S. President Eisenhower spoke to the American Society of [Newspaper] Editors on the international situation. This speech is supposed to be an answer to the Soviet government's recent statements on the possibility of a peaceful settlement of controversial international questions.

This is precisely the reason for the interest in the President's speech shown in all countries by broad public circles, which have been awaiting the reaction of the leaders of the Anglo-American bloc to the new expression of the U.S.S.R.'s peace-loving aspirations.

There has been a sympathetic response to President Eisenhower's words: "We seek, throughout Asia as throughout the world, a peace that is true and total," as there has been to his statement that "none of these issues, great or small, is insoluble—given only the will to respect the rights of all nations."

The President's words on peace and on the fact that none of the issues is insoluble are, however, contradictory to other statements in this speech.

Those wishing to see in Eisenhower's speech a real desire for peace cannot but ask: Why was it necessary in a speech calling for peace for the President to threaten unequivocally an "atomic war?" Is it possible that such arguments will make the President's speech on peace more convincing? In any event, regarding the Soviet Union, such arguments or, more frankly, such threats never have attained and never can attain their goal.

In his speech the President touched upon a number of international problems of varying significance. But in the final analysis, he devoted his speech mainly to the question of mutual relations with the Soviet Union. He said: "I know of only one question upon which progress waits. It is this: What is the Soviet Union ready to do?" To this he added: "The test of truth is simple. There can be no persuasion but by deeds."

And so? It must be agreed that deeds are more valuable than words.

Let us turn to those important international problems on the correct solution of which the strenghtening of peace depends.

First of all, the Korean question.

Can it be denied that in recent years international circles centered their attention on such questions as the war in Korea and the re-establishment of Korea's national unity? In such matters, as is known, the foreign policy of many states was directed in these years.

The Soviet people have invariably supported all steps directed toward concluding a just truce in Korea. The Soviet government immediately supported the recent proposal of the governments of the Chinese People's Republic and the Korean People's Democratic Republic, which offered a new opportunity for passing from words to deeds and opened prospects for ending the Korean war.

Those who seek concrete answers—not words, but actions—for a solution of the urgent problems of international relations can evaluate the significance of this fact.

Let us turn to other international problems.

Who can forget, for instance, the German question or dismiss with general phrases such an important international problem as the re-establishment of Germany's national unity on democratic and peace-loving principles? Who can be satisfied, not only in Germany but beyond its borders, with an approach to this problem by one state or another whereby, let us say, the western part of Germany is merely considered a tool of "dynamic" foreign policy in Europe and no account is taken of the way certain European peoples will react to this, above all the French people, who have more than once been the victim of militarist Germany?

Is it not clear that a solution of the German problem demands consideration of the vital interests of all of Germany's neighbors and the interests of strengthening peace in Europe, and above all the indispensable consideration of the German people's national aspirations?

There is no basis for a solution to this problem in the U.S. President's speech. He did not consider the existence of the four-power Potsdam Agreements on the German problem. The previous U.S. government acted in the same way. If, however, one admits the reasonable necessity for a positive settlement of the German problem in a spirit of strengthening peace in Europe, for which the Soviet Union is unswervingly striving, one cannot forget the above-mentioned important international agreements, signed by both our states and Great Britain and also by France, which joined in these agreements.

If the Anglo-American bloc does not take this into consideration and continues on its projected path, after making the national unification of Germany impossible and after turning Germany's Western part into a militarist state in which power remains in the hands of the revanchists, a fatal mistake will have been made, primarily in regard to the German people. Furthermore, such a stand on the German question is incompatible with the interests of all peace-loving European states and of all progressive mankind.

The issue involved is to conclude a peace treaty with Germany as rapidly as possible, enabling the German people to reunite into a single state and to take their proper place in the community of peace-loving nations, and then to withdraw the occupation forces from Germany, the maintenance of which is an added burden to the German people.

In the U.S. President's statements, which touched upon a wide range of international questions, nothing was said about the Chinese People's Republic, the restoration of China's national rights in the United Nations, or of its legal territorial rights, including the island of Taiwan. Does not this question relate to the urgent international problems of our times? And yet the fact remains that the problem of China was not clarified in this major speech. This means that in regard to China there is a persistent policy motivated by the desire to turn inexorably unfolding events backwards, although every perceptive person realizes that such a policy is doomed to inevitable failure.

In his speech Eisenhower formulated five "precepts" which, according to him, determine "U.S. conduct in world affairs." These "precepts" state that "all humanity hungers for peace, fellowship and justice;" that "any nation's right to a form of government and an economic system of its own choosing is inalienable;" that "any nation's attempt to dictate to other nations their form of government is indefensible," etc.

If these principles really determined U.S. policy and if they were not merely general declarations, they should have had an influence both in regard to the Korean question and to Germany, and to China as well. The fact of the matter is that the declarations are not supported by deeds, that actual U.S. policy to date has paid scant attention to similar declarations in the settlement of these and many other questions.

The President's statement devotes special attention to the peoples of Eastern Europe. It follows from his words that the forms of government in East European countries have been allegedly forced upon them from without, although this contradicts the generally known facts and the true situation in these countries.

The facts show that only by a stubborn struggle for their rights did the peoples of Eastern Europe attain the present people's democratic form of government and that only under the new conditions have they been able to assure vigorous economic and cultural development in their states. It would be strange to expect the Soviet Union to interfere in favor of restoring the reactionary regimes overthrown by these peoples.

At the same time the President simply ignores a commonly known historical phenomenon when he "calls upon" the leadership of the Soviet Union "to use its decisive influence in the Communist world" to retard the liberation movement of the colonial and semicolonial peoples in Asia against their age-old oppression and enslavement. It is difficult to expect a correct understanding of international problems while the national liberation movement is viewed as resulting from the inspiration of "ill-intentioned" individuals.

It is altogether impossible to understand the President's reference to granting "other nations, including those in Eastern Europe," freedom to unite with other countries in a "world-wide community of law." Everybody knows who is blocking the entry of certain people's democracies into the U.N. and who is preventing the restoration of great China's legal rights in the U.N. Was it not the Soviet representatives who proposed to admit 14 countries to the U.N., a proposal rejected by the votes of the Anglo-U.S. bloc?

As for an Austrian treaty, it can be said of it that here too there are no questions which could not be solved on the basis of prior agreement reached with genuine regard for the Austrian people's democratic rights.

Regarding the United Nations.

The President in his speech expressed readiness to make the U.N. an institution capable of effectively safeguarding peace and the security of all peoples.

It is not the fault of the Soviet Union that this organization is not now fulfilling the tasks assigned to it. However, it is not too late to increase the importance of its work even now, particularly in the task of consolidating peace and international security, which was the primary aim of creating this organization.

For this purpose it is above all essential that the principles of the U.N. should be observed by all its members and that the very foundations of its Charter should not be violated. It is also essential that no government try to make the U.N. a tool of its own foreign policy, because this is neither compatible with the principles of the U.N. nor with the aims of defending the interests of normal international cooperation and the consolidation of peace.

For what purpose, one may ask, have all 60 members of the United Nations signed its Charter, a most important part of which is the rule of unanimity of the five great powers in the Security Council when considering problems of ensuring peace? Certainly not in order that this right, recognized by all countries, be ignored in practice by some states, and, of course, not for the purpose of regarding this international principle as some kind of burden or obstacle to the work of the U.N. and the Security Council.

Finally, who can consider as normal a situation in which the largest country in the world, China, is deprived of the possibility of participating in the work of the Security Council and the General Assembly, while instead a Kuomintang scarecrow pops up in U.N. agencies?

Can such a situation contribute to strengthening the authority of the U.N.? In such conditions can one expect a normal development of the United Nations' work and the performance of its duties in consolidating peace and international security?

In any case one cannot evade solving this problem and several other immediate international problems. If we all strive for fewer words and more deeds, it will obviously be possible to find a way to solving such problems as well.

It is not without a reason that in his statement the President has linked the question of reducing armaments with the necessity of devoting more serious attention to economic problems, to problems of combating poverty and need. However, it is unlikely that anyone will be satisfied if this matter is reduced to setting up some kind of "fund for world aid," which was mentioned in this statement.

A high-sounding name alone is not enough for such a "fund."

The results will be different if the approach to such a problem is founded on genuinely broad and democratic cooperation among countries, with full respect for the sovereign rights of peoples and without imposing political conditions upon the countries receiving help.

What the President said about a "fund for world aid" has so far created the impression that we have here a new variant of the Marshall Plan, which failed to justify itself, and at the same time the continuation, under a different name, of the unpopular "Truman's Point Four," which, by doling out pennies to various weak states, tried to subordinate the budgets and the economy of separate countries and colonial territories, and hence these countries and territories themselves, to the so-called "dynamic" aims of U.S. foreign policy. It is evident that the aim now is to proceed further along this same path.

One cannot disregard the fact that recently matters have gone so far as direct refusal of American economic "aid," as in the case of Burma and a number of other countries.

It is also a well-known fact that several countries have lately made explicit statements that they are interested not so much in so-called "aid" from the U.S.A., as in the U.S.A. not placing more and more obstacles to the development of normal trade among states, to the expansion of international trade.

Matters have gone so far that even in countries adhering to the bloc headed by the U.S.A., especially in Britain, protests against restrictions dictated by the U.S.A. on trade with states in the democratic camp are growing louder and louder.

The appeals for peace in the President's speech will, of course, receive our due support. However, it is difficult to close one's eyes to the fact that U.S. foreign policy is as yet far from these peace appeals. The commentaries on the President's speech, for example, which were made only two days after Eisenhower had spoken, by such an authoritative figure as U.S. Secretary of State Dulles vividly confirm this.

One cannot but agree with the speech by former British Labor government Minister Strachey, who described Dulles' speech as an effort to turn Eisenhower's speech into an "act of war."

Dulles shed light to a certain extent upon the fact, which has astounded everybody, that Eisenhower made no mention of China in his speech. It appears that the U.S. government is worried about the fate of so-called "nationalist" China, i.e., the Chiang Kai-shek renegades thrown out of the country by the Chinese people as the result of their victorious struggle. As for the real nationalist China and its sole legal people's democratic government, Dulles even regards it a merit of the U.S. government that it has organized a political and economic blockade of the Chinese People's Republic.

Dulles' belligerence has been known for a long time. It may be that his comment is a somewhat free interpretation of the President's speech, but one cannot disregard the fact that he heads the U.S. State Department and that, whether he will or no, his words are linked to the official point of view of the government headed by Eisenhower.

We cannot therefore ignore Dulles' assertion that the Soviet leaders' appeal for a peaceful settlement of controversial issues was made under pressure of the so-called firm policy of the U.S.A. The whole world knows, however, that the Soviet heads determine their actions not out of consideration for the "hardness" or "softness" of the policy of various countries in regard to the U.S.S.R., but out of consideration for the basic interests of the Soviet people, for the interests of peace and international security.

Although the belligerent pose, of which Dulles is so fond, may seem effective to some people, it hardly reaches its goal, particularly in the field of diplomacy. By linking the possibility of introducing peaceful proposals by the U.S.A. with the formation of the so-called "European Defense Community," with the plans for the organization of "joint armed forces, including French and German forces," i.e., with a further armaments race, Dulles, possibly contrary to his own will, gave away the real meaning of the policy pursued by the U.S.A. But if the real meaning of Eisenhower's statement is what was represented in Dulles' more detailed speech, delivered after the President's, before the same audience and in the same hall, it cannot produce positive results from the point of view of the interests of strengthening peace.

In view of such statements by official U.S. representatives, it is difficult to judge what the foreign political attitude of the U.S. actually is at the present moment. Does it intend to follow the path of relieving tension in international relations and to solve controversial issues on the basis of respect for other people's rights, or does it intend to continue the former policy of an armaments race.

Soviet leaders feel that proposals truly aimed at peace can serve as a basis for improving international relations. This, however, does not mean that Soviet leaders are ready to accept new versions of old methods as such proposals.

In his statement President Eisenhower turned to the results of the postwar period, beginning with the moment when "in the spring of victory the soldiers of the Western Allies met the soldiers of Russia in the center of Europe."

Dwelling on these results, Eisenhower stressed that after the end of the war the countries of the world became divided and followed two distinct roads. At the same time, in complete contradiction to the facts, Eisenhower presents the case as if the countries of the Anglo-American bloc aimed at strengthening peace and international security, while the Soviet Union and the countries with which it maintains friendly relations refused to follow this path. He can even be understood as meaning that the restoration of the war-torn economy and the strengthening of the Soviet Union's economic might in the postwar period began to constitute a new threat of aggression.

To arrive at such assertions in regard to the U.S.S.R. means, at the very least, to lose one's sense of objectivity and to fail to consider well-known circumstances which fully testify not only to the peaceful aims of our country, but also to the fact that the Soviet Union was and is the main bulwark and basic factor in the maintenance and strengthening of world peace.

Such statements were made by the President obviously with the aim of representing the policy of the Anglo-American bloc in a peace-loving light. However, the facts and figures quoted by him on U.S. military expenditures, which are extremely inflated and increasing from one year to the next, tell another story.

These facts testify to unprecedented militarization of the entire U.S. economy, to an excessive burden of military expenditure on the people; they prove that the armaments race in the U.S.A. has created an atmosphere of fear and extreme tension in the country. This policy of the U.S.A., promoting the growth of war hysteria, is pushing a number of other countries along the same road as well.

Eisenhower spoke about the vast expenditure of the U.S. government for guns and rockets, for bombers and fighters, for destroyers and other warships, not forgetting to praise the aggressive Atlantic Pact in doing so. Yet it is known that the policy inspired by the North Atlantic Pact means ever-increasing, colossal military expenditure. It suffices to mention the vast expenditure of funds collected from the American taxpayer for the construction and maintenance of military bases thousands of kilometers away from the U.S.A., in particular on territories to be used for aggressive purposes against the U.S.S.R.

The President cited the cost of a destroyer, a fighter, a bomber, etc., and how many bushels of wheat and tons of cotton could be saved or how many schools or hospitals could be built by giving up the production of such military objects. Not a few instructive figures were cited. But what the President said was entirely inadequate. Had the U.S. President said what it costs the American people to stockpile atom bombs and to build hundreds of military bases far from the borders of the U.S.A.—and after all this has nothing to do with the defense interests of the U.S.A.—he would have provided a picture much closer to reality and considerably more instructive. But it is evident that it is "inconvenient" or "disadvantageous" to talk about all this openly and clearly. Nevertheless, the real meaning of such facts is clear anyhow. They express a foreign policy which pursues unattainable aims of world domination, which is evoking growing resistance from broad circles in many countries.

As for our country, it is known that the Soviet Union, in its unswerving concern with postwar reconstruction and development of its own national economy, has not embarked upon an armaments race. Not only has the Soviet Union not taken this path, it has repeatedly made concrete proposals that the great powers, together with other states, adopt decisive measures for restricting armaments and immediately curtailing armed forces and military expenditures and at the same time agree to prohibit atomic weapons, with the establishment of an effective international control over all these measures to exclude the possibility of violation of these decisions by any state.

In his speech Eisenhower also dwells on the problem of reducing armaments. He devoted five corresponding points to this problem. The Soviet side, of course, does not object to the proposals laid down in these points. All these proposals, however, are of too general a nature and can in no way advance the urgent matter of reducing armaments.

According to Eisenhower, the U.S. government has allegedly always advocated a reduction of armaments while the Soviet Union has taken the opposite position and all but interfered with it.

In this one can detect attempts to blame the Soviet Union for the armaments race conducted in recent years in the countries of the Anglo-American bloc. These attempts, however, have no foundation whatsoever and express only a desire to shift the blame from the guilty to the innocent.

Indeed, was it in the Soviet Union that the war in Korea and the armaments race were heralded as profitable "business," as the best means to ensure business activity and full employment? Is it in the Soviet Union that the so-called "fear of peace" exists, where shares drop on the stock exchange after reports of an easing of tension in international relations? All this happens not in the Soviet Union but in the U.S.A. And what has the Soviet Union to do with this? It needs no armaments race; it always stood and will continue to stand for a stable and lasting peace and has no fear of peace.

Eisenhower, of course, is right in saying that after the victory over Hitlerite Germany the ways of the U.S.S.R. and the U.S.A. parted. But this fact received incorrect and, one could even say, distorted treatment in Eisenhower's statement of April 16.

If one remains on the firm ground of facts, any vagueness in this matter will completely disappear. One cannot, after all, ignore the fact that the countries of the Anglo-American bloc, allies of the U.S.S.R. during the second world war, changed the direction of their policy immediately after the end of this war. In many ways they have turned back to the old, prewar path when their attitude to the Soviet Union could not in any way have been called friendly and when their policy, as a rule, ran in the opposite direction.

We have no intention of entering into a discussion with the President on the rather strange statement about the end of a certain era in Soviet policy. But we cannot accept without surprise his conclusion that the Soviet government must supposedly give up succession in its foreign policy, the correctness of which has been proved by the entire course of international development.

If one connects the beginning or end of an era with the appearance of new persons at the head of one state or another, we have more reason to speak about the end of an era in the policy of the U.S.A. in connection with the advent to power of the Eisenhower government. But for some reason the new U.S. President himself unconditionally defends the entire policy of his predecessor, whom at one time, particularly during the election campaign, he had not unjustly criticized on many accounts.

In his statement the President proclaimed readiness to "welcome any genuine evidence of peaceful purpose." At the same time he asked: "What is the Soviet Union ready to do?"

It is a known fact that the Soviet Union has always shown readiness to discuss and settle, in a friendly manner, immediate international questions, provided that proposals for their settlement, whichever party originates them, are to some extent acceptable and do not run counter either to the fundamental interests of the Soviet people or the interests of other peace-loving peoples.

In his speech the President of the U.S.A. deemed it possible for some reason to link his proposals for peace with a whole series of preliminary conditions imposed by him on the Soviet Union, although these claims in his speech were not strengthened by corresponding obligations on the part of the U.S.A.

Such a way of raising the question has already evoked a just rebuff in the most varied international circles. It could not fail to astonish people capable of a realistic evaluation, both of the essence of immediate international problems and the actual relationship of forces and factors determining the international situation. The British newspaper *Times* has correctly remarked that "no country, be it the U.S.S.R., the U.S.A. or Britain, would be willing to discuss peaceful measures on unconditional terms."

It is known that Soviet leaders are not connecting their appeal for a peaceful settlement of international problems with any preliminary demands on the U.S.A. or any other countries which have or have not joined the Anglo-U.S. bloc. Does this mean that the Soviet side has no claims? Of course not. Despite this, Soviet leaders will welcome any step of the U.S. government or that of any other country if it is directed toward a friendly settlement of controversial issues. This testifies to the readiness of the Soviet side for a serious, businesslike discussion of problems both by direct negotiations and, when necessary, within the framework of the U.N.

The President stated that in solving controversial international issues the "U.S.A. is ready to assume its just part." This statement was not supported in any way in Eisenhower's statement of April 16. Yet, it needs such support.

As for the U.S.S.R., there are no grounds for doubting its readiness to assume a proportionate share in settling controversial international issues. The Soviet Union has proved this on more than one occasion in serious international matters.

Such is the international situation as it looks today.

The policy pursued by the Soviet Union cannot conflict with the interests of other peace-loving states. It answers the aspirations of all states ready to contribute to the development of international cooperation regardless of social system. This policy of the U.S.S.R. at the same time expresses the innermost desires of our people to strengthen world peace.

BOHLEN TO WASHINGTON, APRIL 25, 1953

The full page statement on President's speech and the publication of the speech itself without deletions or any attempt to soften the vigor of the comment on Soviet policies are in themselves events of great importance and in my experience unparalleled in the Soviet Union since the institution of the Stalinist dictatorship. The article itself will require further careful study.

The following preliminary comments are those which on first examination appear to us to merit special mention in addition to points mentioned in Embassy telegram 1526:

1. A great deal of thought and care have obviously gone into the preparation of this article and it is not (rpt not) surprising from its contents that it took a week to compose although possibly the timing of the publication may have been fixed to coincide with the end of the NATO meeting in Paris.

2. It bears evidence of a group composition. Certain variations in style as well as the construction of some sentences appear to reflect the work of several individuals.

3. The name of Stalin does not (rpt not) appear and in describing

162

the Soviet Government the words "Soviet leaders" in the plural are most frequently used.

4. The article is cautious and wary even to the point of indecision and may reflect either the uncertainty of the present leadership or a compromise of differing views with it.

5. The document is not (rpt not) primarily designed for mass propaganda purposes. It is too long and subtle for effective and simple exploitation. Individual phrases (although these are also surprisingly few) can and probably will be selected for emphasis and exploitation by the Soviet and Communist propaganda.

In general the article appears to be designed to serve the following main purposes:

A. To avoid the appearance of throwing cold water on any prospects of peaceful solution and improved relations initiated by President.

B. An attempt to shift the onus placed on the Soviet Union by the President's remarks for the present state of the world back on to the US and its allies. The weakness and, in Soviet terms, mildness of the rebuttal (with the exception of the attacks on the Secretary) plus the publication in full of the President's accurate and trenchant criticism of Soviet policies are striking in the light of past Soviet reaction to any criticism.

C. An attempt to toss the ball back to the United States by declaring that the "Soviet leaders would welcome any step from the US Government" etc., and a rather clear preference for the use of diplomatic channels over those of the United Nations.

D. As already reported, the article gives no (rpt no) new information or clue concerning future Soviet positions in regard to specific subjects listed by President.

It is the Embassy's opinion and also of members of Diplomatic Corps with whom we have had an opportunity to discuss the subject that in this public exchange the United States has come out distinctly the winner. Some reaction from the US Government will of course be necessary without too long a delay. However, in our view while obviously the Soviet reply to the President's speech is not (rpt not) satisfactory or sufficiently definite to give any clear indication of their future policies, we believe it desirable to avoid having the exchange degenerate except by Soviet choice into a propaganda battle, especially since as matters now stand the advantage seems to us to lie with us. We believe it would keep the present Soviet leadership more off-balance and help force them to reveal more of their real purposes if US official comment continues to follow present line inaugurated by President's speech.

Department repeat to other posts in its discretion.

BOHLEN

BB:AW/9
Note: Passed Paris 4/25/53, 1 p.m., HEF
Note: Mr. Bonbright (EUR) notified 2:30 p.m. 4/25/53 FMH.

Appendix N

Churchill and Attlee on Eisenhower's Speech

[*Note*: These extracts bearing on Eisenhower's speech are taken from statements in the House of Commons on May 11, 1953, by Winston Churchill and on May 12 by Clement Attlee. (From *Vital Speeches of the Day* 19, no. 17, June 15, 1953, pp. 522–529.)]

Churchill

The supreme event which has occurred since we last had a debate on foreign affairs is, of course, the change of attitude and, as we all hope, of mood which has taken place in the Soviet domains and particularly in the Kremlin since the death of Stalin. We, on both sides of the House, have watched this with profound attention. It is the policy of Her Majesty's Government to avoid by every means in their power doing anything or saying anything which could check any favourable reaction that may be taking place and to welcome every sign of improvement in our relations with Russia.

We have been encouraged by a series of amicable gestures on the part of the new Soviet Government. These have so far taken the form of leaving off doing things which we have not been doing to them. It is, therefore, difficult to find specific cases with which to match their actions. If, however, any such cases can be cited they will certainly be examined by Her Majesty's Government with urgency and sympathy. On this subject I will now, however, venture to make some general observations which, I hope, will be studied with tolerance and indulgence.

It would, I think, be a mistake to assume that nothing can be settled with Soviet Russia unless or until everything is settled. A settlement of two or three of our difficulties would be an important gain to every peace-loving country. For instance, peace in Korea, the conclusion of an Austrian Treaty—these might lead to an easement in our relations for the next few years, which might in itself open new prospects to the security and prosperity of all nations and every continent.

Therefore, I think it would be a mistake to try to map things out too much in detail and expect that the grave, fundamental issues which divide the Communist and non-Communist parts of the world could be settled at a stroke by a single comprehensive agreement. Piece-meal solutions of individual problems should not be disdained or improvidently put aside. It certainly would do no harm, if, for a while, each side looked about for things to do which would be agreeable instead of being disagreeable to each other.

Above all, it would be a pity if the natural desire to reach a general settlement of international policy were to impede any spontaneous and healthy evolution which may be taking place inside Russia. I have regarded some of the internal manifestations and the apparent change of mood as far more important and significant than what has happened outside. I am anxious that nothing in the presentation of foreign policy by the N.A.T.O. Powers should, as it were, supersede or take the emphasis out of what may be a profound movement of Russian feeling.

We all desire that the Russian people should take the high place in world affairs which is their due without feeling anxiety about their own security. I do not believe that the immense problem of reconciling the security of Russia with the freedom and safety of Western Europe is insoluble. Indeed, if the United Nations organization had the authority and character for which its creators hoped, it would be solved already.

The Locarno Treaty of 1925 has been in mind. It was the highest point we reached between the wars. As Chancellor of the Exchequer in those days I was closely acquainted with it. It was based upon the simple provision that if Germany attacked France we should stand with the French, and if France attacked Germany we should stand with the Germans.

The scene today, its scale and its factors, is widely different, and yet I have a feeling that the master thought which animated Locarno might well play its part between Germany and Russia in the minds of those whose prime ambition it is to consolidate the peace of Europe as the key to the peace of mankind. Russia has a right to feel assured that as far as arrangements can run the terrible events of the Hitler invasion will never be repeated, and that Poland will remain a friendly Power and a buffer, though not, I trust, a puppet State.

I venture to read to the House again some words which I wrote exactly eight years ago, 29th April, 1945, in a telegram I sent to Mr. Stalin:

"There is not much comfort"

I said,

"in looking into a future where you and the countries you dominate, plus the Communist Parties in many other States, are all drawn up on one side, and those who rally to the English speaking nations and their associates or Dominions are on the other. It is quite obvious that their quarrel would tear the world to pieces, and that all of us leading men on either side who had anything to do with that would be shamed before history. Even embarking on a long period of suspicions, of abuse and counter-abuse, and of opposing policies would be a disaster hampering the great developments of world prosperity for the masses which are attainable only by our trinity. I hope there is no word or phrase in this outpouring of my heart to you which unwittingly gives offense. If so, let me know. But do not, I beg you, my friend Stalin, underrate the divergencies which are opening about matters, which you may think are small to us but which are symbolic of the way the English-speaking democracies look at life." I feel exactly the same about it today.

I must make it plain that, in spite of all the uncertainties and confusion in which world affairs are plunged, I believe that a conference on the highest level should take place between the leading Powers without long delay. This conference should not be overhung by a ponderous or rigid agenda, or led into mazes and jungles of technical details, zealously contested by hordes of experts and officials drawn up in vast, cumbrous array. The conference should be confined to the smallest number of Powers and persons possible.

It should meet with a measure of informality and a still greater measure of privacy and seclusion. It might well be that no hard-faced agreements would be reached, but there might be a general feeling among those gathered together that they might do something better than tear the human race, including themselves, into bits.

For instance, they might be attracted, as President Eisenhower has shown himself to be, and as "Pravda" does not challenge, by the idea of letting the weary, toiling masses of mankind enter upon the best spell of good fortune, fair play, well-being, leisure and harmless happiness that has ever been within their reach or even within their dreams.

I only say that this might happen, and I do not see why anyone should be frightened at having a try for it. If there is not at the summit of the nations the will to win the greatest prize and the greatest honour ever offered to mankind, doom-laden responsibility will fall upon those who now possess the power to decide. At the worst the participants in the meeting would have established more intimate contacts. At the best we might have a generation of peace.

I have now finished my survey of the world scene as I see it and as I feel about it today. I express my thanks to the House for the great consideration with which I have been treated. I hope I have contributed a few thoughts which may make for peace and help a gentler breeze to blow upon this weary earth. But there is one thing I have to say before I end, and without it all the hopes I have ventured to indulge would be utterly vain. Whatever differences of opinion may be between friends and allies about particular problems or the general scale of values and sense of proportion which we should adopt, there is one fact which stands out over-whelmingly in its simplicity and force. If it is made good every hope is pardonable. If it is not made good all hopes fall together.

This would be the most fatal moment for the free nations to relax their comradeship and preparations. To fail to maintain our defense efforts up to the limit of our strength would be to paralyze every beneficial tendency towards peace both in Europe and in Asia. For us to become divided among ourselves because of divergencies of opinion or local interests, or to slacken our combined efforts would be to end for ever such new hope as may have broken upon mankind and lead instead to their general ruin and enslavement. Unity, vigilance and fidelity are the only foundations upon which hope can live.

Attlee

I am inclined to agree with the Prime Minister that perhaps the most significant thing has been the change in internal policy in Russia. I notice today in "The Times" a quotation from "Pravda" which was headed "Collective Leadership." There does seem to be a definite departure from the autocracy of Stalin, and it rather confirms the view that many of us held that Stalin was, in fact, the master of Russian policy. Today, there is, at all events, something different, something more like a collecting of the voices of a number of men.

A further point on which I am very much in agreement with the Prime Minister is that "piecemeal solutions of individual problems should not be disdained or improvidently put aside."

There is great danger in trying to go out with a too-wide objective. When the logs are jammed in the river one must begin by extricating a single log, or one or two logs, in the hope that thereby the whole mass may move. Particularly here, we want to aim to get closer personal relationships. I do not know whether the right hon. Gentleman or other Members of Her Majesty's Government have ever met Mr. Malenkov. I have not, to my knowledge. My knowledge of the leaders of Russia is confined now to Mr. Molotov, Mr. Vyshinsky and Mr. Kaganovitch. What we want to get is greater understanding, by us of them and by them of us. It would be a great thing if we could get personal relations which would dissipate some of the Soviet mythology about Britain.

Another point by the Prime Minister which struck me as wise was that one should not assume that all the troubles of the world are due to Communist initiative. I have no illusions as to the activities of the Comintern, but the fact is that there are other movements in the world as well. The Prime Minister cited the case of the Viet Minh attack in Laos. No doubt there is a policy whereby Soviet Russia, for its own purposes, supports every nationalist movement, but that does not mean that there are no genuine nationalist movements of which we have to take account whether they are in Indo-China, Egypt, Arabia or, for that matter, in Africa. It really is an overall simplifying of the problem to put it all down to Soviet intrigue. There is a body of opinion in the United States and some in this country that tend to do just that thing. On the other hand, there are people in this country and elsewhere who tend to put down all our troubles to American policy. That, too, is a mistake.

It is worth while saying a few words about the United States and about American policy. I hope they will cause no offense. I hope that no one will suggest that I am in any way anti-American. I have very many friends in America and I worked in great harmony with President Truman and his advisors. I am very conscious of all that the Americans have done for the world, besides in the war. Nor do I wish to attack the American Constitution. I merely want to state some facts which do not always seem to be apprehended. Let me begin with a contrast.

The Prime Minister comes to the House and states his policy. It is the policy of the government. He can, if he wishes, get a vote in this House in support of it or he can, as in this debate, be satisfied with the great measure of support on both sides. That policy is Government policy and will be carried out by Ministers and by officials. Look on the other side. President Eisenhower makes a great speech. It is the President's speech. He speaks for the Administration, but in America power is divided between the Administration and Congress. For instance, the Administration may desire to spend so many billions in support whether of armaments or some other object, but Congress may cut it down by several millions of dollars. The Administration may wish to encourage our export to the United States but, as in the case of the Chief Joseph Dam, influences frustrate the Administration's policy.

Therefore, the Government in America are not really master in their own house. Let us remember, too, that Congress is still made up of people who primarily represent the interests of a particular State in the Union. Pressure groups and interests are very strong and, further, the American Administration seems to be less integrated than ours. President Eisenhower makes a speech; shortly thereafter the Secretary of State Mr. Dulles makes a speech, which, I thought, struck rather a different note. We do find on occasions that there is one policy being run by the Treasury, another by the State Department, and perhaps another by the Pentagon.

A further point seems that the American tradition is to give their representatives overseas a freer hand than we give ours, and less direction. We found rather the same in the relationship, as compared with our chiefs of staffs and our commanders in the field, between the American chiefs of staffs and their generals in the field. I am not complaining. It is just the American tradition. Therefore, we find that General Harrison, in the Panmunjom negotiations, seems to make observations on his own, right off his own bat, and even makes a broadcast. One wants to face these facts.

One of the facts of the world situation is that the American Constitution was framed for an isolationist State. Americans did not want to have anything to do with Europe. For many years they had practically no foreign policy, but I do not think that that situation is particularly well suited to a time when America has become the strongest State in the world and has to give a lead. I am not in any way criticising the Americans or the Constitution. I am endeavouring to state facts, because I think that people often are misled and there are misunderstandings and disappointments because we do not understand the American Constitution. . . .

I turn for a moment to Europe. I have only a very few words to say. My right hon Friend the Member for Greenock (Mr. McNeil) will be speaking in the debate and will be dealing with this matter at greater length. We have to face up to this German problem. The fact is that East Germany is heavily armed and Western Germany is not armed. We desire a united Germany, but a united democratic Germany. There is a danger that if we join these two parts of Germany when one part is controlled by a faction which is heavily armed, democracy might not last long in Germany.

It is essential that in dealing with the German problem we should continue to deal with it from strength, by building up our N.A.T.O. forces. On the other hand, looking broadly at this problem, I think it is a mistake to suggest that a united Germany should automatically be part of N.A.T.O. The Russians are bound to object to that, just as we should object if it were suggested that Western Germany should become a satellite of the Russian Empire. We laid down certain conditions with regard to German rearmament. They deal with the contributions Western Germany might make for our common defense, but if we get a united Germany and set up a Government there, that Government will have to decide what they are going to do.

The Prime Minister invoked Locarno. I remember Locarno, and

the Locarno spirit. I am not altogether clear what this would amount to in practice. I should rather like to hear it further developed. I was not quite sure how, in the present world, the various parts in the drama of Locarno were assigned; but it is a suggestion. I have one word to say about the Austrian Treaty. Soviet Russia would make a tremendous gesture if she could agree to the Austrian Treaty.

With regard to a conference on the highest level, I agree with the Prime Minister that it would not be advisable to stage a conference with an enormous retinue of experts. I am sure that anything in the way of public discussions would be a mistake. We have seen that at U.N.O. I would say, however, that any such conference needs most careful preparation. We want to be sure what we want, and that applies not only to this country but to the United States of America.

I want to advert to that point for one moment because there, again, we have the peculiar Constitutional position of America. It would be possible for President Eisenhower to attend a conference and, on his return to the United States, to be thrown over, as President Wilson was after the discussions at Versailles. It is, therefore, essential that whoever goes to this conference should go with full authority. We need full co-operation in searching out these ideas. We should be unwise—I think the Prime Minister would agree—to expect that that conference would dramatically clear up all international difficulties. Its chief value would be in getting personal contacts and understanding, from which a careful building up of peace might ensue.

We have had a number of remarkable speeches and pronouncements in recent weeks. We have had the speech of President Eisenhower. We had the "Pravda" article, which showed some signs of thaw in the frozen region of the relationships of Russia with the Western world. I am quite sure that the Prime Minister's speech has made a valuable contribution, and I think this House has, too, because I think the speeches of yesterday were kept at a high level of debate, and I am quite certain that Great Britain still has the power and the will to give a lead for peace.

Appendix O

Two Accounts of the Foreign Ministers Meeting in Berlin on February 10, 1954

[*Note*: This appendix contains one exuberant and one professional account of Molotov's performance at the foreign ministers meeting in Berlin on February 10, 1954. The former is from a letter of the same day from C. D. Jackson to an unnamed correspondent (from the C. D. Jackson Papers, box 27, "Berlin Basics and Working Papers" folder, Dwight D. Eisenhower Library); the latter is Anthony Eden's terse report to his cabinet colleagues on February 11 (from *Full Circle*, p. 82).]

Jackson

This has been the most dramatic day yet. I will try to give a blow-by-blow but don't think I can do justice to it. You have to hear the sound, see the faces change from pleasure to pain and vice versa, feel the danger of looming booby traps and get the thrill of coming through with the enemy visibly shaken.

Yesterday had definitely been our round. Molotov had talked interminably and said nothing new. When Foster Dulles, next in turn, very quietly said, "I have heard nothing new. I have nothing to say", the Russians were thrown off base and started whispering to each other. Then Bidault and Eden both felt called upon to say something, which gave Molotov a chance at another round. When he was finally cornered he pulled out what we had been expecting all along, the announcement that he would present a formal Soviet proposal for European Security.

All evening and part of the night and this morning we were trying to dope out what it would consist of. The boys had it pretty well taped, although they could not guess that having succeeded in embarrassing us, Molotov would throw the whole thing away and give us the greatest chance we have had thus far. By two incautious or arrogant or just ill-informed (I don't know which) statements, the tide of battle swung right around and we nailed him so hard that I don't think he will be able to squirm out of it.

The beauty of the nailing is not just the satisfaction of scoring in the meeting. The real victory is that in one package he has been made to alienate East and West Germans, and, most importantly, the slightly neutralist SPD, plus the French, plus the British, plus anybody who wants to listen.

Molotov was in the chair and asked if he could talk first. The chair generally calls on the person to his left to open, but everyone agreed and Molotov started a long harangue on Germany and European security, winding up with a specific plan for the unification of Germany and a draft of a collective security treaty for Europe.

We were feeling less and less happy, because although his proposals were phony all through, nevertheless they contained bits and pieces that could not help but have appeal to the French and the Germans—withdrawal of troops, neutralization of Germany, and a lot of subtle little twists that might look good to the folks in Paris or the Socialists in East Germany, etc. etc. EDC was roundly denounced, but NATO was left vague.

Then came the block buster. The U.S. was specifically excluded from the collective security pact but was permitted to be an "observer" along with communist China. At that point we all laughed out loud and the Russians were taken completely by surprise at our reaction. Molotov did a double take and finally managed a smile, but the Russian momentum was gone.

When he was through, he turned to Dulles, who was next to speak. Dulles said that this was something new and complicated and asked for a twenty minute recess for study, and we all filed out.

Dulles, Bidault, and Eden got together for about ten minutes, and then Dulles had another ten minutes with his staff, and we went back feeling that we were in a tight spot, but that we might get out of it. One of the reasons for our uneasiness was that Dulles had simply listened to the advice that everybody was tossing at him but had not given any indication that things had jelled in his mind.

Personally, I didn't think they could possibly have jelled, because there had not been enough time.

He started very slowly, literally sentence by sentence, with long pauses while it was translated first into Russian and then into French. This was one of the rare times when consecutive translation was a blessing. Generally it interferes with the effect; this time it accentuated it.

As he got into it we all realized that he was on exactly the right pitch, leaving to the Europeans the job of defending the U.S. presence in Europe and NATO and sticking to those matters of history and principle which would force Bidault and Eden to close ranks.

When he got toward the end there wasn't a sound in the room. By that time he was pausing between paragraphs instead of sentences so that the final paragraph stood out in letters of gold. When he said that every country could make its own choice, but that the United States would not be absorbed, I almost bawled, and I am sure a lot of others felt the same way.

Then came Bidault who was superb, and then Eden who put the lid on it by saying very simply that the proposal was "unacceptable".

The whole Russian house of cards had come tumbling down, and it could be seen on the Russian faces. Molotov was drawn, gray and angry, and they were all scribbling furiously and avoiding looking up in our direction, which they always do when they think they are doing well. This business of Russian omniscience and omnipotence in conference is nonsense. They are so rigid and inflexible that if one comma gets knocked out of place they don't know what to do. That is somewhat of an exaggeration as Molotov is agile, but even he can't take two paragraphs being knocked out of place.

Molotov's rebuttal was pathetic and almost ruined him because he had practically to admit that his plan called for the liquidation of NATO, which is the one thing France and England *know* is their salvation. He also admitted that his scheme would probably perpetuate the division of Germany for 50 years, which certainly will endear him to his German audiences and he also admitted that this business of troop withdrawal was a phoney because the Russians could come back any time they wanted, literally without any pretext other than the unilateral announcement that they felt like coming back.

Finally, when Foster, toward the end, said that classifying the

Americans as "observers" may be considered by some a poor joke, but by Americans as an affront after the blood and treasure the U.S. had expended in Europe, Molotov actually went white and then red.

We have maintained an advantage up to now, sometimes precarious, sometimes solid. I think that today has won the battle of Molotov's momentary bulge and that he won't be able to reform his forces.

The session lasted from 3 to 8:15, and then some of us went to the opera, arriving in the middle of the second act. When the audience spotted Dulles during the intermission, everyone rose to his feet, applauding wildly and shouting, "Mr. Dulles, Mr. Dulles, Mr. Dulles". Tremendously moving.

This has been a day. My net reaction is that I am damn proud to be an American and that I know we will win.

Eden

Yesterday was by far the worst day in discussions here, in that Molotov showed his hand more unashamedly. It is now perfectly evident that the objective of the Soviet attack is not merely E.D.C., but N.A.T.O. and the whole Western defense system. As I mentioned before I left London, they plan to entice all Europe under the slogan: "Europe for the Europeans." The so-called European Security Pact would in my judgment result in the free countries of Western Europe enjoying the same independence and security as Hungary, Poland, etc.

I do not think we can do any good by discussing Soviet demands for the abolition of N.A.T.O. in public, and I am more than ever convinced that the sooner this conference ends its discussion of the German side of our affairs the better. I will do my best to this end.

Notes

1. A substantial number of secondary works have examined the president's speech before the American Society of Newspaper Editors on April 16, 1953, and its relationship to the Soviet "peace offensive" following Stalin's death. Richard P. Stebbins, *The United States in World Affairs, 1953* (New York: Harper and Brothers, 1955), pp. 105–108, 114–132, describes in considerable detail the crucial events of March and April 1953. Both Robert J. Donovan, *Eisenhower: The Inside Story* (New York: Harper and Brothers, 1956), pp. 72–76, and presidential assistant Sherman Adams, *Firsthand Report* (New York: Harper and Brothers, 1961), pp. 95–98, also deal briefly with that period. Richard Goold-Adams, *The Time of Power: A Reappraisal of John Foster Dulles* (London: Weidenfeld and Nicolson, 1962), pp. 85–86, 109–119, concentrates upon what he views as the essentially negative and obstructionist role played by Secretary Dulles.

   President Eisenhower's version of the events leading to the speech is contained in his *Mandate for Change, 1953–1956* (Garden City: Doubleday, 1963), pp. 143–149. One of the most detailed accounts of the often agonizing drafting and redrafting of the speech can be found in Emmet John Hughes, *The Ordeal of Power* (New York: Atheneum, 1963), pp. 100–115. For some reason Hughes begins his account only in "mid March," although he was intimately involved from the March 6 draft forward; but his version contains much valuable information. Another useful participant's account of the administration's immediate response to Stalin's death is Robert

Cutler, *No Time for Rest* (Boston: Little, Brown and Company, 1965), pp. 320–323.

Louis L. Gerson, *John Foster Dulles*, in Robert H. Ferrell (ed.), *The American Secretaries of State and Their Diplomacy* (New York: Cooper Square Publishers, 1967), pp. 128–131, examines Dulles' role with greater sympathy than that found in Goold-Adams' work. However, both Townsend Hoopes, *The Devil and John Foster Dulles* (Boston: Little, Brown and Company, 1973), pp. 170–175, 180, and Leonard Mosley, *Dulles: A Biography of Eleanor, Allen and John Foster Dulles and Their Family Network* (New York: Dial Press, 1978), pp. 330–338, share Goold-Adams' view that the secretary of state harbored scant enthusiasm for an American peace overture to Stalin's successors.

Several general works on the Eisenhower period examine the administration's reaction to the Soviet dictator's death. A concise and generally accurate account is Herbert S. Parmet, *Eisenhower and the American Crusades* (New York: Macmillan Company, 1972), pp. 274–281. Peter Lyon, *Eisenhower: Portrait of the Hero*, second edition (Boston: Little, Brown and Company, 1974), pp. 530–534; Charles C. Alexander, *Holding the Line: The Eisenhower Era, 1952–1961* (Bloomington: Indiana University Press, 1975), pp. 65–66; and Elmo Richardson, *The Presidency of Dwight Eisenhower* (Lawrence, Kans.: Regents Press, 1979), pp. 61–62, also provide useful information.

2. Statement of March 15, in *Pravda*, March 16, 1953; *Current Digest of the Soviet Press* 5, no. 8, April 4, 1953, p. 5.
3. Adams, *Firsthand Report*, p. 97.
4. Monnet's account of the evolution of the EDC, from the attack on South Korea to its failure in the French assembly on August 30, 1954, is to be found in his *Memoirs* (Garden City: Doubleday, 1978), pp. 336–362, 368, 381–382, 394–399.
5. Ibid., p. 396.
6. Konrad Adenauer, *Memoirs, 1945–53*, trans. Beate Ruhm von Oppen (Chicago: Regnery, 1966), pp. 430–434.
7. Interview by Don North, December 17, 1970. J. F. Dulles Oral History Project, Seeley G. Mudd Manuscript Library, Prince-

ton University; transcripts available at the Eisenhower Library. The image is also evoked by Bohlen in his *Witness to History, 1929–1969* (New York: W. W. Norton, 1973), p. 311. Bohlen notes that he made the remark half jokingly to someone who repeated it to Dulles, who, presumably, was not amused.

8. John W. Hanes, Jr., personal aide to Dulles, puts this point well in a letter to me of February 20, 1981, commenting on an earlier draft of this book:

> [Dulles] had been profoundly influenced by what he considered to be the failure of a number of his predecessors and specifically including Dean Acheson to be able to translate much of their foreign policy decisions into effective American governmental policy, because of a failure to gain congressional support (and, sometimes, because of having to endure active congressional hostility). He was determined to do his best not to let this happen to President Eisenhower and himself.
>
> Both he and President Eisenhower, from their separate experiences, were more aware than most men in Washington of the shortcomings, with respect to foreign policy, of what you describe as the "Republican Right", especially in the Senate—and, particularly, of the danger represented by a demagogue as personified by Joe McCarthy (who, I think, cannot properly be described in terms such as "right" or "left"). But, especially in 1953, these things existed; they were influential in the Senate (and beyond); and they could not be ignored as forces.

9. Bohlen, *Witness to History*, pp. 311–312.
10. See especially ibid., Chapter 18, pp. 309–336.
11. John W. Ford, member of the Foreign Service and an extraordinarily courageous security officer at the time, records the climax of the Bohlen affair as follows ("The McCarthy Years inside the State Department," *Foreign Service Journal*, November 1980, p. 12):

> Senator Joseph McCarthy and certain other members of Congress questioned the nomination by the Eisenhower

administration of Chip Bohlen to be the next ambassador to the Soviet Union. The so-called "evidence" on which to question his appointment took several forms: innuendoes in his security file or in FBI reports—the "raw" material which so frequently constitutes part of basic background investigations. The most highly advertised bit of "evidence" was a tape recording, allegedly containing Ambassador Bohlen's voice. This tape purportedly implicated him in activities which made him a security risk. Secretary Dulles called me to his office, where the security office file and the FBI reports on Ambassador Bohlen were assembled on his conference table. I was instructed to bring a tape recorder.

As I entered Secretary Dulles's office, I was introduced to Senators Taft and Sparkman. The secretary, with a flourish, instructed me to review with the senators the files on Mr. Bohlen. The secretary noted, however, that allowing the senators to see these files was "without prejudice to the concept of executive privilege."

Neither senator found anything incriminating in the files and then we proceeded with the tape recording. Unfortunately the extension cord for the recorder was too short, the quality of the tape was poor and the volume potential of the recorder was low. This means that Senators Taft and Sparkman and I had to lie down on the floor of Secretary Dulles's office in front of his desk and listen to the recording. I certified in a document that it was not Ambassador Bohlen's voice. That was also evident to all present. Shortly thereafter Ambassador Bohlen was cleared and took off for his new assignment.

12. This paraphrase is from C. J. V. Murphy, "The Eisenhower Shift," *Fortune*, January 1956.
13. Donovan, *Eisenhower*, pp. 108–109.
14. W. W. Rostow, in collaboration with Alfred Levin and with the assistance of others, *The Dynamics of Soviet Society* (New York: W. W. Norton, 1953). See especially pp. 244–245, 251–252.

15. Ibid., p. 252.
16. See George F. Kennan, *Memoirs, 1925–1950* (Boston: Little, Brown, 1967), especially pp. 415–466, and *Memoirs, 1950–1963* (Boston: Little, Brown, 1972), especially pp. 3, 39–54, 90–104, 131–144, 159–162.
17. Kennan, *Memoirs, 1925–1950*, pp. 462–464. On pp. 446–448 Kennan, with admirable candor, lays out, with hindsight, certain assumptions in his earlier argument which were proved false.
18. For an account of the development and fate of this paper, see ibid., pp. 415–448.
19. Kennan's interview in the J. F. Dulles Oral History Project indicates that Bohlen, as well as Jackson, asked him to come to Washington to discuss "questions arising from Stalin's death."
20. Philip E. Mosely, "The Kremlin's Foreign Policy since Stalin," *Foreign Affairs* 32, no. 1 (October 1953): 20, 22.
21. Gerson, *Dulles*, pp. 129–130. Gerson evidently had access to diplomatic exchanges which have not yet been fully declassified.
22. Adenauer's full analysis is to be found in *Memoirs*, pp. 434–435, and in the account of his trip to the United States, pp. 438–455. The extracts in the text are from pp. 438, 442, 444, and 455.
23. Goold-Adams, *Time of Power*, p. 110.
24. The three memoranda of conversations on p. 53 are to be found in the John Foster Dulles Papers, Telephone Call Series, box 10, "White House Telephone Conversations, Jan.–April, 1953" folder, Dwight D. Eisenhower Library. In his letter of February 20, 1981, responding to a draft of this book, John Hanes supplied the following useful account of the origin and limitations of these memoranda:

  I think I should make a comment about the memoranda. . . . As a routine matter, the Secretary's phone conversations were monitored by his personal assistant (Burnita O'Day in the beginning, subsequently Phyllis Bernau—

now Phyllis Macomber). Burnita or Phyllis would make shorthand notes; and later, when she had time, would put these notes down in memorandum form, primarily so that Rod O'Connor or I (the only others who read the memoranda) could pick up any matter requiring action and see that suitable action was taken by the appropriate person. The purpose of these memoranda, therefore, was primarily operational; and while both Burnita and Phyllis made every effort to be accurate and complete in their transcription, neither they, nor Rod or I, were worried as to the accuracy of nuance or detail. Frequently, the subject being discussed would be one as to which the transcriber was not personally familiar, or involved matters, persons or relationships of which she had no knowledge.

These memoranda were almost never read by the Secretary (there was no reason for him to do so); and they went into the files precisely as written, having served their original operational purpose, and remaining solely as a convenient reference of the time and date of various calls. Even if one contained an actual (inadvertent) error, it would not have been corrected by any of us. We were not trying to record history.

They are an invaluable source of information; but they should be utilized with an understanding of their origins, their intended purpose, and, therefore, their limitations.

An exception of the foregoing comment is that the Secretary's conversations with the President were never monitored, except on those rare occasions when, at the Secretary's specific direction, his assistant would get on the line to take down something specific that the President wanted to say to him. The memoranda of conversations with the President, therefore, always emanated from the Secretary himself—usually dictated by him; rather rarely, dictated either by Rod or myself from what he had told us. This latter event would be only when he was too pressed for time to dictate himself, or feared he might forget something if he waited until he had time;

in these cases, we always submitted such a memorandum to him, usually for his initials, but at least for his knowledge and approval of its contents.

Hanes later reported to me (June 30, 1981), after checking with Phyllis Bernau Macomber, that the practice of monitoring telephone conversations between Eisenhower and Dulles was somewhat more common than his earlier account, above, would suggest.

25. Hughes, *Ordeal of Power*, pp. 102–104. Hughes' full account of the origins and development of the speech, as he saw it, is on pp. 100–115. Several commentators on a draft of this book expressed reservations about the use of Hughes' long direct quotation of what Eisenhower said on March 16, 1953. There is every reason to believe from subsequent speech drafts and the transcript of the Hughes-Dulles conversation of the same day (pp. 56–57) that Eisenhower spoke in the vein Hughes evokes. It is the literal precision of the quotation that was questioned. Hughes did not make available to the author his diary in the Mudd Library at Princeton where, presumably, the occasion was reported at the time. I am, nevertheless, inclined to believe Eisenhower laid out his views as Hughes reports them.

26. See Note 24, above.

27. C. D. Jackson Papers, box 85, "Stalin's Death Speech" folder, Dwight D. Eisenhower Library.

28. Hughes, *Ordeal of Power*, pp. 117–118.

29. Churchill had, in fact, twice raised again the question of a four-power meeting in the immediate aftermath of the president's speech: in a brief statement before the House of Commons on April 20 and in a message to Eisenhower on April 22. Eisenhower replied on April 25 in a letter including this paragraph:

> As to the next step, I feel that we should not rush things too much and should await the Soviet reply or reaction longer than a few days. There is some feeling here also for a meeting between Heads of States and Governments, but I do not think this should be allowed to press us into

precipitate initiatives. Premature action by us in that direction might have the effect of giving the Soviets an easy way out of the position in which I think they are now placed. We have so far seen no concrete Soviet actions which would indicate their willingness to perform in connection with larger issues. In the circumstances we would risk raising hopes of progress toward an accommodation which would be unjustified. This is not to say, of course, that I do not envisage the possible desirability at an appropriate time that the three Western Powers and the Soviets come together. We should by all means be alert.

30. Harold Macmillan, *Tides of Fortune, 1945–1955* (New York: Harper and Row, 1969), p. 511.

31. The foreign ministers conference held in Berlin during January and February 1954 has generated a modest amount of historical controversy, especially regarding the role played by Secretary of State John Foster Dulles. Richard P. Stebbins, *The United States in World Affairs, 1954* (New York: Harper and Brothers, 1956), pp. 114–128, provides an excellent narrative of the proceedings and concludes that Soviet intransigence was the principal reason for the conference's general lack of success. John Robinson Beal, *John Foster Dulles* (New York: Harper and Brothers, 1957), pp. 185–203, is extremely laudatory regarding Dulles' actions at Berlin. Beal regards the secretary's performance as a highlight of his long public career. According to Beal, Dulles skillfully thwarted Soviet efforts to divide the Western powers and also won the propaganda contest, demonstrating to world opinion that it was the Soviet Union, not the United States, that blocked a European settlement. A less favorable view is advanced by Goold-Adams, *Time of Power*, pp. 111–113.

David J. Dallin, *Soviet Foreign Policy after Stalin* (Philadelphia: J. B. Lippincott, 1961), p. 141, presents an effective summary of the apparent tactics pursued by the Russian delegation at Berlin. Also useful in this regard is Adam B. Ulam, *Expansion and Coexistence: Soviet Foreign Policy, 1917–*

1973, second edition (New York: Praeger, 1974), pp. 51–52. Both authors concede, however, that, in the absence of documents from the Kremlin archives, conclusions about actual Soviet tactics must remain highly speculative.

A detailed account of the diplomatic sparring that accompanied the Berlin conference is included in Anthony Eden's memoirs, *Full Circle* (Boston: Houghton Mifflin, 1960), pp. 66–85. Eden, who attended the sessions in his capacity as British foreign secretary, concludes that the Soviets viewed the conference both as a propaganda forum and as a final opportunity to divide the West over EDC and German unity. A similar conclusion is expressed in Eisenhower, *Mandate for Change*, pp. 342–344, and Macmillan, *Tides of Fortune*, pp. 528–530. The evidence in Eisenhower's memoirs suggests that neither the president nor his secretary of state expected any substantive achievements from the Berlin meeting. Consequently, they were primarily concerned about preventing a Russian propaganda triumph and countering any Soviet moves to create dissension within the NATO alliance.

There are several brief treatments of particular aspects of the Berlin conference. Charles E. Bohlen, who attended the meeting as one of Dulles' advisers, offers some general observations concerning the secretary's actions in his *Witness to History*, pp. 362–363. Sven Allard, *Russia and the Austrian State Treaty* (University Park: Pennsylvania State University Press, 1970), pp. 115–119, concentrates on those sessions that dealt with the status of Austria and its relationship to the more difficult German issue. Townsend Hoopes, *The Devil and John Foster Dulles*, pp. 205–206, and Peter Lyon, *Eisenhower*, pp. 595–596, examine the conference primarily from the standpoint of its connection with the subsequent Geneva conference on Indo-China. Both authors also sharply criticize most of the negotiating positions adopted by Dulles throughout the Berlin proceedings.

32. The Berlin conference was the kind of occasion when Dulles, by all accounts, was most comfortable and, in human terms, at his best: completely focused on a single problem, surrounded by a small, supportive group of aides, in unambiguous com-

mand. In letters of February 1, 1954, to an unnamed recipient and February 9, 1954, to Robert Cutler, C. D. Jackson commented:

> Foster is also very good at working with his staff. He consults them constantly and listens and frequently takes suggestions contradicting his ideas without a quiver.
> I suspect that this is the kind of existence he loves and because he is enjoying it, his personality is blossoming. . . . Particularly interesting to me is the fact that his relations with his staff are very warm and human, with lots of humor and great understanding of the other fellow's problems. Furthermore, his background press conferences have been models of interesting informative lucidity.
> Are you beginning to think by now that I have gone soft?

Both letters are from the C. D. Jackson Papers, box 27, "Berlin Basics and Working Papers" folder, Dwight D. Eisenhower Library.

33. The Bohlen interview is from the J. F. Dulles Oral History Project in the Seeley G. Mudd Manuscript Library, Princeton University. Bohlen's more measured statement of his retrospective view is in *Witness to History*, p. 371:

> Looking back, I believe I was remiss at the time of Stalin's death in not recommending that Eisenhower take up Churchill's call for a "meeting at the summit"—the first time this phrase was used—with Malenkov. Dulles batted down the idea. I was not asked for an opinion and doubt that I would have been listened to if I had expressed one at that time. Dulles had told the senators he did not want me as an adviser. But I think I made a mistake in not taking the initiative and recommending such a meeting.
> After the death of Stalin, there might have been opportunities for an adjustment of some of the outstanding questions, particularly regarding Germany. In addition to the extraordinary act of *Pravda*'s publishing the text of a speech by President Eisenhower calling for peace, the Soviet press let up on its hysterical Hate America

campaign. May Day slogans—a clue to the Bolshevik line of thinking—showed a striking contrast to those published for the anniversary of the Bolshevik Revolution the preceding November, when Stalin was still living. Instead of "down with the warmongers" and references to "imperialist aggressors" and "foreign usurpers," there were expressions of confidence in the ability to resolve all differences between nations. Soon after his assumption of power, Malenkov himself said in a statement that there were no issues that could not be negotiated. Khrushchev subsequently charged that Malenkov and Beria had been contemplating a change in Soviet policy on Germany, possibly relinquishing the hold on East Germany and permitting some form of unification in return for a demilitarized, neutralized Germany. Khrushchev, as he often did, was undoubtedly stretching the truth. I doubt if any Soviet leader ever seriously contemplated giving up the Sovietized area of Germany. But there might have been room for some other accommodation.

34. Goold-Adams, *Time of Power*, p. 119.
35. The possibility that the post-Stalin leadership may have been willing, for a transient interval, to contemplate a good-faith negotiation leading to an all-German settlement remains an unresolved historical question. Those scholars who contend that Kremlin policy regarding the German question moderated significantly between March and June 1953 base their argument on two factors. Some cite the Soviet government's more conciliatory rhetoric and actions on a wide range of issues following Stalin's death. Others concentrate on the shadowy foreign policy activities of Lavrenti P. Beria, who supposedly favored a policy of détente with the West, including an all-German settlement. In both cases, the evidence is indecisive and the issue remains one for speculation rather than dogmatism.

Lyon, *Eisenhower*, pp. 531–534, and Mosley, *Dulles*, pp. 337–338, argue that the new Soviet leadership was ready for serious discussions concerning disputes with the West. In their view, the United States missed an excellent opportunity to reduce East-West tensions by not responding to Russian peace initiatives sooner and with greater flexibility.

The primary evidence supporting the thesis of a Beria plan to accept a unified, non-Communist Germany is a subsequent accusation to that effect against Beria by Nikita Khrushchev published in the *New York Times*, March 11, 1963, pp. 1 and 9, and March 16, 1963, p. 18. If Khrushchev's 1963 speech were the only evidence of such a plan, it might well be dismissed as nothing more than a crude attempt by the Soviet leader to discredit a long-dead adversary. However, speculation concerning Beria's conciliatory goal existed even in 1953. Mosely, "The Kremlin's Foreign Policy since Stalin," pp. 24–25, noted several signs that the Soviet government had relaxed its most onerous controls and was urging its German client state to adopt a less combative posture toward the West. Mosely speculated that Beria and his German protégé, Wilhelm Zaisser, hoped to make the East German regime more respectable in preparation for all-German negotiations.

Two of the most detailed and persuasive works advancing the thesis that Beria intended to abandon East Germany are Boris I. Nicolaevsky, "The Meaning of the Beria Affair" (December 1953), in Janet D. Zagoria (ed.), *Power and the Soviet Elite: "The Letter of an Old Bolshevik," and Other Essays by Boris I. Nicolaevsky* (New York: Frederick A. Praeger, 1965), pp. 126, 135–137, 146, and Wolfgang Leonhard, *The Kremlin since Stalin* (New York: Frederick A. Praeger, 1962), pp. 70–73. Leonhard's arguments are the most intriguing since he relies, in part, on the testimony of two high-level East German defectors. Also relevant in the discussion of the "abandonment" issue are David J. Dallin, *Soviet Foreign Policy after Stalin*, pp. 171–179; Walter Laqueur, *Russia and Germany: A Century of Conflict* (London: Weidenfeld and Nicolson, 1965), pp. 277–278; Arnold L. Horelick and Myron Rush, *Strategic Power and Soviet Foreign Policy* (Chicago: University of Chicago Press, 1966), pp. 26–30; Robert G. Wesson, *Soviet Foreign Policy in Perspective* (Homewood, Ill.: Dorsey Press, 1969), pp. 219–220; Thomas W. Wolfe, *Soviet Power and Europe, 1945–1970* (Baltimore: Johns

Hopkins University Press, 1970), p. 77; and Adam B. Ulam, *Expansion and Coexistence*, p. 543. Most of these authors, especially Dallin, Laqueur, Wesson, and Ulam, view with considerable skepticism the notion that Beria or any other Soviet leader would have advocated a policy of abandonment with regard to the East German regime.

36. *Wall Street Journal*, April 29, 1980. For the author's non-authoritative reply to Arbatov, see the *Wall Street Journal*, May 8. Both pieces were published on the editorial page.

37. Eisenhower, *Mandate for Change*, pp. 503–505.

38. Richard H. Immerman cites a 1956 example of Eisenhower's instructing Dulles to avoid, in the context of the Suez crisis, "a long wearisome negotiation, especially with an anticipated probability of negative results in the end." See his "Eisenhower and Dulles: Who Made the Decisions?" *Political Psychology* 1, no. 2 (Autumn 1979): 27.

39. Several close observers have noted in interviews in the J. F. Dulles Oral History Project that the Eisenhower-Dulles relationship changed with the passage of time. For example, James Hagerty, Rod O'Connor, and Emmet Hughes agree that the early months of the relationship were the most uncertain, as Dulles learned to accommodate to the style of his new client. They also agree that, with the passage of time, Dulles' confidence in the relationship increased—although, as the next two volumes in this series will suggest, elements of uneasiness persisted down to 1955 at least. Stalin's death and the ensuing debates and activities within the administration occurred in the early shakedown months. The question raised is whether this fact significantly affected the policies pursued by the United States. Without dogmatism, I am inclined to believe that Eisenhower's 1953 reservations about summitry, as well as Dulles', were quite deeply rooted as were their instinctive differences with respect to the appropriate tone to be adopted at such a juncture. I would guess that transient uncertainties in their working relationship played no significant role in the outcome.

40. Three examples of this gap between presidential posture and subsequent governmental performance were Eisenhower's

proposals at the 1955 Geneva summit (to be explored in the next book of this series); the passages on aid to developing nations in his second inaugural address (to be explored in the book after that); and his proposals for organizing development aid in the Middle East in his August 1958 Lebanon-Jordan speech before the United Nations General Assembly.

41. Quoted in Immerman, "Eisenhower and Dulles," p. 28.

42. Ibid., p. 18.

43. I wrote the following about C. D. Jackson in 1961 when a small book in tribute was assembled on the occasion of a dinner organized in his honor and in support of one of his favorite charities. See John Mason Brown (ed.), *C. D. Jackson: A Personal Journal* (New York: Children's Asthma Research Institute and Hospital, 1961), p. 63.

> It is almost a decade now that I have had the privilege of knowing C. D. and engaging side by side with him in various enterprises which we both believed to be good. As all his friends know, C. D. is one of the most courageous, imaginative and dedicated men of his generation. His wisdom and high seriousness are joined with an underlying modesty and tempered by a sense of humor which few crusaders command.
>
> When the history of the past decade is written, even C. D.'s friends will be surprised to know how many of the enterprises of which the nation can be proud were sparked or colored by his initiative. I recall a day in March, 1953, when C. D. came out of a high-level meeting in Washington and announced: "I don't know whether I'm carrying my shield or on it." In these matters we all have batting averages; but he has emerged carrying his shield many more times than most. And I trust he will continue for many years to come.
>
> I have known no gayer or more loyal companion in a good fight.

I would not alter these words for this quite different occasion.

44. Kennan, *Memoirs, 1925–1950*, p. 446. Although not directly germane to the present argument, the balance of this passage from Kennan (pp. 446–447) is worth quoting:

Where we really differed was over such things as the need for the retention of greater negotiating flexibility in our relations with the Russians—the need for not permitting a new West German government to become an end in itself and thus an enduring impediment to any agreement with Russia—the need for more searching and less formal exploration with our French and British allies of the problem of the future of the European continent—the weight to be given to the views of a military occupational establishment which I regarded as both politically illiterate and corrupted by the misleading discipline of its own experience. These disagreements reflected the differences in our respective backgrounds. He, having never lived in Eastern Europe or Russia (and perhaps sharing Sigmund Freud's view that the people east of the Elbe were "baptized late and very badly"), considered the possibility of agreement with the Russians on the retirement of Russian forces from the Eastern zone of Germany to be of relatively small importance and thus expendable, whereas our occupational establishment in Western Germany, and the Western unity it symbolized, were definitely not. I, on the other hand, haunted by memories of long residence in both Germany and Russia, considered our occupational establishment in Western Germany decidedly expendable, but clung desperately to the hope of getting the Russians to retire some day from the heart of the continent, and fought to prevent our adopting a stance which threatened to destroy every possibility of such a retirement for an indefinite number of years to come.

As noted earlier (p. 44), Kennan's view and its background differed to a degree from Jackson's and mine. What we shared was a judgment that a lifting from Eastern and Central Europe of Soviet occupation and the lifting from all of Europe of a military confrontation on the Elbe were objectives worthy of great and imaginative effort which, we felt, could be reconciled with a holding of the West together, should the effort fail.

45. The file does indicate that Emmet Hughes, White House speech writer, was among the five officers of the government who supplied some input or commentary to Dulles' April 18 speech.
46. C. D. Jackson Papers, box 56, "Log 1955," Dwight D. Eisenhower Library.
47. Quoted in Immerman, "Eisenhower and Dulles," pp. 35–36.

Index

7, 49, 57, 61–63, 65, 67, 69–
70, 72–76, 78, 84, 90, 95
Big Three summit meeting, 64–65,
74, 95
Bohlen, Charles E., analysis of
Izvestia and *Pravda* editorials,
62, 162–164; and Big Four summit meeting proposal, 70, 72,
186n; confirmation of, 20; and
Council of Foreign Ministers
meeting, 185n; and Dulles,
70, 179n, 185n–187n; and
Eisenhower, 18, 20, 186n; and
Europe, Eastern, 40; and Jack-
son, 105; and Kennan, 45, 181n;
and McCarthy, 20, 179n–180n;
and Princeton conference,
40–41; and State Department,
18–20, 28, 106; and US peace
initiative, 5, 104–106, 186n
Bonn, 6, 15
Brazil, 128
Brewster, Kingman, 45
Brown, John Mason, 190n
Brussels, 15
Brussels Pact, 10, 16–17, 67
Budget Bureau, 24
Bulganin, Nikolai A., 97
Bulgaria, 16
Bundy, McGeorge, 45
Burma, 17–18, 156
Byrnes, James F., 80

Cambridge, Mass., 45, 104, 106,
109, 142
Canada, 10, 13, 42
Captive Nations Resolution, 62
Center for International Studies
(CENIS), 35–40, 45, 102–103,
106
Central Intelligence Agency (CIA),
and CENIS, 35, 102–103; and
NSC, 35; and Stalin's death, 3,
96–101
Chief Joseph Dam, 170
China, 17–18, 59, 90, 138, 153
China, Nationalist, 59; and China,

People's Republic of, 59, 153,
157; and UN, 155; and US, 125,
129, 132, 138, 153, 157; and
USSR, 153, 155, 157
China, People's Republic of, and
China, Nationalist, 59, 153, 157;
and European Security Pact,
174; and France, 126; and Geneva conference, 67; and Indo-
china, 18, 67, 126; and Korean
War, 17, 21, 152; and UN, 153–
155; and US, 57, 62, 125–
126, 153–154, 157; and USSR,
57, 66, 100, 152–154, 157
Churchill, Winston S., and arms
race, 64; and Attlee, 169, 172;
and Austria, 63, 166; Big Four
summit meeting, 7, 49, 63,
69–70, 73–76, 167–168, 183n,
186n; Big Three summit meeting, 64; as Chancellor of the Exchequer, 166; and Dulles, 64,
78; and Eisenhower, 7, 48–49,
62, 64, 70, 73–75, 93–95, 168,
183n–184n, 186n; and Europe,
Western, 166; GDR, 71; and Germany, 52; and Korean War, 63,
166; Locarno Treaty, 166; and
NATO, 166; and Poland, 167;
speech on peace initiatives,
165–169; and Stalin, 49, 165,
167; and US peace initiative,
48–49, 58, 62–64, 106, 165–
169; and USSR, 49, 63, 69, 75,
165–167
Clay, Lucius D., 81
Clayton, Will L., 80
Cold War, 27–38, 41, 62, 73, 136,
144–145
Columbia University, 28
Cominform, 16–17, 62, 131
Comintern, 37, 169
Communism, in Asia, 17–18, 100,
126, 154; in France, 16; international, 28, 98–100; in Italy, 16;
in Latin America, 126–127; in
Middle East, 126–127

194

and Allied Control Council, Berlin, 33; and arms control, 34, 54–58, 60, 75, 117, 120, 155, 159–160; and arms race, 25–26, 33, 54–57, 75, 116–117, 151, 159–160; and Atoms for Peace, 65; and Attlee, 63–64, 169–172; and Big Four summit proposals, 7, 49, 69–70, 73–74, 84, 95, 183n–184n, 186n, 189n; and Big Three summit meeting, 49, 64; and Bohlen, 20, 186n; budget of, 21–26, 33, 72; and China, 125; and Churchill, 7, 48–49, 62–64, 70, 74–75, 93–95, 168, 183n–184n, 186n; and Council of Foreign Ministers, 6, 108, 112; and Dulles, A., 57; and Dulles, J. F., 8–9, 19, 46, 51, 53, 57, 69–70, 73, 75, 78–82, 132–133, 182n–183n, 185n, 189n; and economic policy of, 21–26, 33, 72; and Europe, 3, 9, 60, 116, 120, 127–128, 153–154, 158; foreign policy of, 3, 6–9, 22–26, 41, 46–47, 60, 72–75, 109, 113–133; and France, 7, 84; on Free World, 118; and Geneva conference, 190n; and Germany, 3, 8–9, 52, 120; and Great Equation, 22–26, 33; and Hughes, 54, 56–58, 183n; and Jackson, C. D., 3–4, 41, 57, 70, 75–77; and Jackson, W., 102; and Korean War, 7, 9, 21–22, 24, 26, 33, 60, 118–119, 122, 125; Library, 84, 96, 111, 138, 140, 148, 150, 173, 179n, 183n, 186n, 192n; and Mayer, 48; and Middle East, 190n; military career of, 74–75, 80; military policy of, 21–26, 33, 60, 72, 92–93, 115–117; and NATO, 14; on press, 114; and prisoners of war, 138; and psychological warfare, 32–33, 75–76, 102; and Repub-lican party, 21, 26, 74, 179n; and role of federal government, 23–26; and Second World War, 114–115, 158; speech of April 16, 1953, 8–9, 48–49, 61, 64, 69–70, 73, 75, 80, 102, 109, 113–123, 142, 148, 150–162, 168, 170, 172, 177n, 186n; and Stalin, 3, 9, 38–39, 72, 118, 134, 136–137; and State Department, 18–19, 112, 129; and Suez crisis, 189n; and UK, 7, 48–49, 84; and UN, 56–57, 65, 190n; and US foreign policy, 115–116, 153; and US peace initiative, attitude toward proposals for, 7–9, 21, 26, 52, 54–56, 69, 73, 75, 80–81, 84; and US peace initia-tive, delay of, 7–8, 70, 109; and US peace initiative, diplomatic follow-up to, 9, 61–68, 70–71, 80, 122–133, 146–149, 156–158, 173–176; and US peace ini-tiative, proposals for, 3–7, 9, 38–39, 45–49, 52–54, 57–60, 84–93, 102–110, 142–146; and US peace initiative, reactions to, 8, 61, 146–147, 150–172; and USSR, 33, 34, 49, 54–56, 73–74, 116–120, 150–151, 158; and USSR, draft of proposed message to, 84–93; and USSR peace initiative, reaction to, 47–48, 50, 53, 150–151, 183n–184n; and Western allies, 4, 7, 48, 51–52, 120, 158; and Wilson, C., 103

Eisenhower, Milton S., 127
Elbe, 10, 44, 191n
Europe, Central, 134–135, 191n
Europe, division of, 9, 42–44, 58, 60, 68, 76, 80, 120, 143–144, 158, 191n
Europe, Eastern, 54, 76; and Dulles, 127; and Eisenhower, 60; and Europe, Central, 135; and Europe, Western, 135; and Euro-

123, 142, 150, 152, 173–176
Freud, Sigmund, 191n

General Electric Corporation, 103
Geneva conference, 67, 72, 81,
  185n, 189n–190n
Germany, 6, 8, 186n; and Austria,
  185n; democracy in, 4, 9, 11–12,
  44, 66, 69, 86, 91, 106, 171; division of, 11, 16, 60, 175; and
  Dulles, 66, 78–79, 82, 123; and
  EDC, 15, 66, 123, 142, 157; and
  Europe, Eastern, 49, 145; and
  Europe, Western, 13, 42, 78,
  134; and France, 13–14, 49, 52,
  69, 110, 123, 145, 152, 166; limitations of power of, 43–44, 49,
  66, 110, 146, 152; and NATO, 14;
  neutralization, 51, 174, 187n;
  occupation of, 44, 174; oil, 83;
  peace treaty, 12, 66, 142, 153;
  and Poland, 167; and prisoners
  of war, 51, 138–139; rearmament of, 11–12, 14, 42, 66, 78,
  143; reunification of, 4, 9, 11–
  13, 15, 26, 37, 39, 41, 43–44,
  48–49, 51–52, 54, 57, 59,
  65–67, 69–73, 78–79, 82, 86,
  91, 106–107, 110, 135, 143,
  145–146, 148, 152–153, 171,
  174–175, 185n, 187n–188n;
  Revolution of 1848, 11; and Stalin, 83; and UK, 166, 171; and
  US, 4, 9, 26, 39, 49, 56, 59,
  72, 86, 91, 93, 106–107, 128,
  143–145, 152–153; and USSR,
  9, 11–14, 16, 39, 48–49, 52,
  59, 65–66, 72–73, 106, 123,
  142–143, 148, 152–153, 167,
  187n–188n
Germany, East (GDR), 171; and Adenauer, 12; and arms limitations
  in, 37; and Beria, 65; Communist control in, 72, 188n; and
  democracy in, 37, 66; economy
  of, 71; and FRG, 12, 71–72, 171;
  and Germany, reunification of,

37, 66, 71, 143; inspection of,
  37; liberalization in, 65, 71–72,
  79; riots in, 9, 64, 70–73; Socialists in, 174; and UK, 71, 171;
  and UN, 12; and USSR, 9, 12, 37,
  64–66, 70–73, 79, 143, 146,
  174, 187n–189n, 191n
Germany, West (FRG), 11–12, 66,
  171; and Adenauer, 12–13, 72,
  143, 146; Bundestag, 15, 49; domestic politics of, 51, 65, 70, 72,
  79, 143; and Dulles, 7, 15, 66,
  78–79, 108; economy of, 13,
  79; and EDC, 14–15, 49, 67,
  109–110, 118, 123, 142–144,
  157; and GDR, 12, 71–72, 143,
  171; and Germany, reunification
  of, 15, 51–52, 66, 78, 110,
  145–146; limitation of power
  of, 144; and NATO, 67, 118; occupation of, 67; and prisoners of
  war, 138–139; rearmament of,
  143–144, 153; and SPD, 12, 15,
  143, 146, 174; and UK, 67, 171;
  and US, 48, 58, 66, 128, 143–
  146, 152–153, 191n; and US
  peace initiative, 6–7, 48, 107,
  132, 145, 146; and USSR, 12,
  17, 50, 51, 78, 110, 142–143,
  152–153, 191n; West, associa-
  tions with, 15, 67, 118; Western
  European Union, 67
Gerson, Louis L., 48–49, 178n,
  181n
Goodpaster, Andrew, 75
Goold-Adams, Richard, 70, 80,
  177n–178n, 181n, 184n, 187n
Great Britain (UK), 42, 161; and
  Austria, 63, 166; and Big Four
  summit meeting proposal, 63,
  167–168, 172; and Big Three
  summit meeting, 49, 64, 84; and
  Canada, 13; and China, People's
  Republic of, 126; and Council
  of Foreign Ministers, 86, 111,
  173–176, 185n; and Dulles, 156;
  and EDC, 143; Europe, Western,

159, 162, 174, 176, 185n; New
Economic Policy, 36; nuclear
weapons, 10, 29–31, 65, 72, 75,
159; October Revolution, 27;
peace initiative of, 4, 7–8, 33,
46–48, 50–51, 53–56, 73,
78–79, 109, 125, 142–144,
150–151, 161, 165–172; and
Philippines, 17; and Poland, 167;
and Popular Front, 36; postwar
recovery of, 16, 30, 83, 91,
158–159; Presidium, 97; and
prisoners of war, 51, 119, 138;
purges in, 27, 36; and Rumania,
48; and Second World War, 28,
33, 37–38, 85–86, 89, 115, 134,
150, 160; security forces of, 100;
security of, 29–30, 36, 60, 85,
89, 98–99, 134, 145, 166; and
Stalin's death, 16, 36–37, 84,
87–89, 96–103, 162–163; Supreme Soviet of, 46; and Truman Doctrine, 16; and Turkey,
16; and UK, 67, 78, 134, 150–
152, 165–176; and UN, 12, 47,
128, 154–155, 162–163, 166;
and US containment policy,
41–43; US peace initiative, 8,
54–56, 62, 71–72, 140–141,
148, 150–164; US test of intentions of, 34, 49, 59, 62, 65, 138;
and Yugoslavia, 16, 100
United Nations (UN), 55, 57, 62,
86, 90, 92–93, 115, 127–128,
131, 172; and arms control, 120;
Charter of, 155; and China,
153–155; and Europe, Western,
166; and GDR, 12; General Assembly of, 12, 52, 54, 65, 84,
108, 155, 190n; and Germany,
12; and Hammarskjöld, 47; and
Korean War, 17, 47, 90, 125;
Security Council of, 90, 155;
and UK, 166, 172; and US, 134,
154–155; and USSR, 12, 47, 128,
154–155, 162–163, 166
United States (US), 161; and Allied

Control Council, Berlin, 33;
arms control, 41, 75, 90–91, 93,
117, 120–121, 135, 159–160;
arms race, 29–31, 91, 116–117,
151, 157–160; and Asia, 9, 119;
and Austria, 4, 41, 56, 86, 91, 93,
119, 138, 154; and Big Four summit proposal, 7, 49, 57, 63, 65,
67, 69–70, 72–76, 78, 84, 90,
95; and Big Three summit meeting, 49, 84, 95; and Brazil, 128;
and Burma, 156; and China, Nationalist, 125–126, 129, 153,
157; and China, People's Republic of, 57, 125–126, 153,
157, 174; and Cold War, 29–34,
38, 41; Congress of, 128–129,
170; Constitution of, 170, 172;
and Council of Foreign Ministers, 65–67, 79, 86, 93, 111–
112, 173–176; economy of, 3,
21–26, 72, 117, 158–160; and
EDC, 4–5, 7–8, 50, 66, 109,
113–125, 142–143, 146, 148–
149; and Europe, division of,
3–4, 9, 42–43, 58, 143, 145,
158; and Europe, Eastern, 9, 40,
42, 58, 120, 122, 143, 145–146;
and Europe, security of, 4, 72,
86, 123–124, 135, 175; and Europe, Western, 9, 11, 42–43, 72,
120, 141, 149; European Security
Pact proposal, 174, 176; and
France, 7, 13, 56, 58, 67, 84, 93,
95, 110, 112, 126, 128, 141, 143,
145–146, 150, 152, 173–176,
191n; and Free World coalition,
86, 93–94, 145; and FRG, 7,
49–50, 58, 72, 109–110, 128,
132, 143, 145–146, 152–153,
191n; and Germany, 8–9, 56, 72,
93, 109–110, 145–146; and Germany, democracy in, 4, 9, 86,
91, 120; and Germany, rearmament of, 11, 13, 110, 143, 152–
153; and Germany, reunification
of, 3–4, 9, 37, 41, 135, 143,